Conceptualize Writer

"I Got a Play for You: A Hustler's Handbook for Serial Entrepreneurs."

First published by Culture Game Publishing 2024

Copyright © 2024 by Conceptualize Writer

All rights reserved. No part of this publication may be reproduced, stored or transmitted in any form or by any means, electronic, mechanical, photocopying, recording, scanning, or otherwise without written permission from the publisher. It is illegal to copy this book, post it to a website, or distribute it by any other means without permission.

Conceptualize Writer has no responsibility for the persistence or accuracy of URLs for external or third-party Internet Websites referred to in this publication and does not guarantee that any content on such Websites is, or will remain, accurate or appropriate.

First edition

This book was professionally typeset on Reedsy
Find out more at reedsy.com

Dedication

This book is dedicated to every hustler, dreamer, and entrepreneur who refuses to let their circumstances define their potential. To the resilient souls in underserved communities who turn challenges into opportunities and struggles into success—you are the heartbeat of innovation and progress.

To my family and close friends, for your unwavering belief in me, your support through the late nights and early mornings, and for reminding me of the power in persistence.

Epigraph

"The true hustler is not defined by how many times they win, but by how many times they rise after a fall. Success isn't a destination, it's a relentless journey fueled by vision, grit, and an unshakable belief in oneself."

– Anonymous

Foreword

Foreword

In today's world, hustling has taken on a whole new meaning. No longer is it just about working hard; it's about working smart, seizing opportunities, and navigating the challenges that come with being an entrepreneur. It's about building something from nothing and finding ways to succeed even when the odds are stacked against you.

"I Got a Play for You: A Hustler's Handbook for Serial Entrepreneurs" is not just another book on entrepreneurship. It's a blueprint for those who understand that success doesn't come easy, especially for those from underserved communities. It's for the dreamers, the grinders, and the visionaries who are willing to put in the work to create something meaningful—something that will leave a lasting impact.

Jamal Woodley, through his own journey, has demonstrated the power of persistence, creativity, and resilience. From navigating industries as diverse as tech, entertainment, and finance, to launching brands in the Web3 space, he has proven that no challenge is insurmountable if you're willing to pivot, adapt, and learn from every experience.

This book is filled with practical advice, real-world examples, and strategies that can help anyone—whether you're just starting out or looking to scale your business—find success. It's about more than just business tactics; it's about cultivating the right mindset to thrive in any industry, building a network that supports your growth, and creating a lasting legacy that goes beyond profit.

Whether you're launching your first startup, managing multiple ventures, or transitioning from a side hustle to a full-time enterprise, this book is for you. Jamal's words are a reminder that while the journey is tough, the rewards of hustling smart and relentlessly are beyond measure. And most importantly, this book gives you the play you need to succeed.

Let the hustle begin.

Preface

Hustling is in my blood. It's something I grew up watching and learning from the people around me—the entrepreneurs, the visionaries, and even those who had to scrape together whatever they could to make things happen. I saw firsthand the grind, the setbacks, and the resilience it took to turn nothing into something. But most of all, I saw the drive to succeed, no matter the odds.

"I Got a Play for You: A Hustler's Handbook for Serial Entrepreneurs" was born out of my own experiences and lessons learned across a wide range of industries—tech, travel, blockchain, publishing, and more. This book isn't just about running a business; it's about navigating the complexities of being an entrepreneur, particularly when you're coming from an underserved community or facing challenges that others might not understand.

This isn't a book of theory. It's a playbook—filled with the strategies, tips, and mindset shifts that helped me build multiple businesses from the ground up. I know what it's like to start with nothing but an idea and an ambition, and I know the work it takes to turn that into something real and sustainable. Whether it was managing cash flow with no traditional banking support or learning how to pivot when things didn't go as planned, every challenge brought with it a lesson.

This book is for those who want more than just advice. It's for those who need real-world strategies that can be applied immediately—whether you're bootstrapping your first venture, building a personal brand, or scaling your hustle into a full-fledged enterprise. It's also for those who are looking to create a legacy, not just for themselves but for their communities.

The hustle isn't easy, but it's worth it. And with the right mindset, the right strategy, and the right play, you can take your business—and your life—to the next level. That's what this book is about: giving you the play you need to win, no matter where you're starting from.

Thank you for picking up this book. I'm excited to share these lessons with you and, more importantly, to see how you take them and run with them in your own journey.

Let's get to work.

Acknowledgments

No journey is ever walked alone, and this book is no different. "I Got a Play for You: A Hustler's Handbook for Serial Entrepreneurs" is the product of countless lessons learned, countless hours spent in the grind, and the unwavering support of a community of people who believed in me even when the odds seemed impossible.

First and foremost, I want to thank my family. Your support, love, and belief in me gave me the strength to keep pushing through every obstacle. To my parents, for instilling in me the work ethic that drives everything I do. To my closest friends, who have been my sounding boards, advisors, and motivators. You've been there for the highs and the lows, and your faith in my vision has kept me going.

To my mentors and business partners, thank you for the wisdom, guidance, and invaluable lessons you've shared with me over the years. Your input has shaped me not only as an entrepreneur but also as a person. I'm grateful for the doors you've helped me open and the paths you've guided me through.

To the MintMade Brands team and everyone within our growing ecosystem, thank you for believing in the vision. This book wouldn't be possible without the hard work and dedication of each of you. You are the living embodiment of what it means to hustle and build something from nothing.

Finally, to the readers of this book—thank you. You are the reason I wrote this, and I'm excited to see how you take the plays laid out in these pages and make them your own. Whether you're just starting out or deep into your hustle, I hope this book gives you the tools and motivation to keep going and never stop believing in your dreams.

This book is for all the hustlers, dreamers, and entrepreneurs out there who refuse to give up. Let's make history together.

– Jamal Woodley

Table of Contents

Table of Contents

1. The Hustle Begins
   - Laying the Foundation for Success in Underserved Communities

2. Identifying Opportunities in the Struggle
   - Turning Challenges into Profitable Ventures

3. The Hustler's Mindset
   - Cultivating Resilience, Creativity, and Relentless Drive

4. Building Your Personal Brand
   - Standing Out in a Crowded Market

5. Navigating the Financial Jungle
   - Managing Money When Traditional Banking Isn't an Option

6. Mastering the Art of Networking
   - Leveraging Connections for Business Growth

7. The Art of the Pivot
   - Adapting and Shifting Strategies to Overcome Obstacles

8. Bootstrapping Your Business
   - Growing with Limited Resources

9. Securing Funding in Unconventional Ways
   - Exploring Microloans, Crowdfunding, and Alternative Capital Sources

10. Digital Hustle: Leveraging Technology
    - Using Apps, Social Media, and Online Platforms to Enhance Your Business

11. Building a Solid Team
    - Assembling the Right People to Support Your Vision

12. Hustling in Multiple Industries
    - Balancing and Succeeding in Diverse Ventures
13. Marketing on a Budget
    - Creative and Cost-Effective Strategies for Getting the Word Out
14. Dealing with Setbacks and Failures
    - Turning Losses into Lessons and Bouncing Back Stronger
15. Scaling Your Hustle
    - Transitioning from a Side Hustle to a Full-Fledged Enterprise
16. Legalizing Your Hustle
    - Understanding Business Registration, Contracts, and Compliance
17. Protecting Your Intellectual Property
    - Safeguarding Your Ideas, Brand, and Products
18. Community Engagement and Giving Back
    - Building Businesses that Benefit the Community
19. Sustaining Success
    - Maintaining Relevance and Innovation Over Time
20. Legacy Building
    - Creating a Lasting Impact and Planning for the Future

I
Part One

1

Chapter 1

Chapter 1: The Hustle Begins

Every great journey starts with a single step, and for a hustler, that step often begins in the most unlikely of places. It's not the boardroom or the classroom where the hustle is born—it's in the streets, in the corners of the community, in the grind of everyday life. Whether you're selling candy in school, flipping sneakers, or running a small side business out of your trunk, the hustle begins when you decide that you won't be confined by your circumstances. You see potential where others see despair, and you're willing to put in the work to turn that potential into profit.

1.1 The Origins of the Hustle

The hustle isn't something you learn in school; it's a mindset cultivated through necessity. Growing up in underserved communities, you quickly realize that the traditional routes to success might not be available to you. Banks don't lend money to people who look like you. Employers might overlook you based on your zip code. But the hustle is about more than survival—it's about thriving, even when the deck is stacked against you. It's about recognizing that while the system might not be built for you, you can still build something for yourself.

1.2 The Importance of Grit

Grit is the cornerstone of the hustle. It's that inner drive that keeps you moving forward, even when the path is unclear and the obstacles seem insurmountable. Grit is waking up at 5 AM to hit the pavement, to make those sales, to meet those clients—day in and day out. It's understanding that nothing worth having comes easy, and the grind is a necessary part of the journey. Grit is what separates those who talk about success from those who achieve it.

1.3 Starting Small, Dreaming Big

One of the most important lessons for any hustler is that it's okay to start small. Too often, people are discouraged by the size of their dreams because they don't have the resources to make them a reality right away. But the hustle is about playing the long game. It's about starting where you are, with what you have, and building from there. Maybe you're selling homemade goods to friends and family, or offering services to your neighborhood. Whatever it is, you're planting the seeds for something bigger. You're learning the ropes, making connections, and most importantly, you're proving to yourself that you can do this.

1.4 Leveraging Your Surroundings

Your community is your first customer base, your first network, and your first source of support. Look around you—what do people need? What are the gaps in your neighborhood? Maybe there's a demand for quality clothing, affordable food options, or reliable car services. The key to a successful hustle is recognizing these needs and figuring out how to meet them in a way that's both profitable for you and valuable to your community.

1.5 The First Steps

So, how do you start? First, you identify your strengths and interests—what are you good at, and what do you enjoy doing? Next, look for opportunities in your immediate environment. Who needs what you have to offer? Start small, set achievable goals, and don't be afraid to take risks. Remember, every successful business started as someone's side hustle. The most important thing is to start. Don't wait for the perfect moment because it doesn't exist. The hustle begins the moment you take that first step.

1.6 Building Momentum

Once you've started, it's all about building momentum. Each sale, each new connection, and each small success adds fuel to your fire. As your confidence grows, so will your hustle. You'll begin to see opportunities that you never noticed before, and you'll gain the experience needed to tackle bigger challenges. The key is to stay consistent, stay hungry, and keep pushing forward. The hustle is a marathon, not a sprint, and every step you take brings you closer to your goals.

In this first chapter, we've laid the groundwork for what it means to be a hustler in underserved communities. The hustle begins with a mindset, a drive, and the willingness to start small and dream big. It's about leveraging your surroundings, taking that first step, and building momentum. As we move forward, we'll dive deeper into the strategies and tactics that will help you turn your hustle into a thriving business. But remember, it all starts here—with the decision to hustle, no matter the odds.

2

Chapter 2

Chapter 2: Identifying Opportunities in the Struggle

The most successful hustlers have one thing in common: they see opportunities where others see obstacles. This chapter is about developing that eye for opportunity, even in the toughest circumstances. It's about turning the challenges you face every day into stepping stones toward your success.

2.1 Seeing Beyond the Struggle

In underserved communities, the struggle is real. Poverty, crime, lack of access to education and healthcare—these are daily realities. But within these challenges lies a wealth of untapped potential. Where others see scarcity, a true hustler sees possibility. The key is to train your mind to look at problems not as dead ends, but as opportunities to innovate and create solutions that people will pay for.

For example, consider the lack of affordable, healthy food options in many urban neighborhoods. This problem is often referred to as a "food desert." But instead of accepting this as a reality, think about how you could solve it. Maybe it's through a small grocery delivery service, or by partnering with local farmers to bring fresh produce to your area. Identifying these kinds of opportunities is the first step in transforming struggle into success.

2.2 Listening to the Community

The best business ideas often come from simply listening to what people around you need. Take the time to engage with your community—talk to your neighbors, your friends, your family. What are their pain points? What do they wish they had that isn't currently available? What services or products do they spend money on outside the community that could be offered locally?

By tuning into these conversations, you can uncover needs that aren't being met and then position yourself as the one who can meet them. This not only sets you up for success but also strengthens your ties to the community, making your business more resilient in the long run.

2.3 Turning Personal Struggles into Opportunities

Sometimes, the best opportunities come from your own personal struggles. What have you faced in your life that was difficult, inconvenient, or unfair? How did you overcome it? There's a good chance that others in your community are facing similar challenges, and they would pay for a solution.

For instance, if you've had trouble finding affordable childcare, consider starting a service that connects parents with trusted local caregivers. Or if you've struggled with transportation, think about ways to provide low-cost rideshare options or even a bike rental service. By turning your own struggles into opportunities, you not only create a viable business but also help others in your community who are facing the same issues.

2.4 Learning from Others' Successes and Failures

Success leaves clues, and so does failure. Look at other businesses, both in your community and beyond. What are the success stories, and what can you learn from them? On the flip side, where have others gone wrong? Maybe a business started strong but couldn't keep up with demand, or perhaps it failed to connect with its target market. Analyzing these factors will help you identify what works and what doesn't, giving you a head start in your own ventures.

Don't just look at traditional businesses, either. Some of the most innovative ideas come from unconventional sources. Keep your eyes open, study your competition, and be willing to learn from their experiences.

2.5 Embracing the Digital World

In today's connected world, technology is a game-changer. The digital space offers endless opportunities to turn a side hustle into a thriving business. Whether it's setting up an online store, using social media to reach new customers, or leveraging apps and services to streamline your operations, embracing technology can amplify your impact.

For example, if you're selling homemade products, platforms like Etsy or Shopify can help you reach customers far beyond your local community. Social media platforms like Instagram and Facebook are powerful tools for marketing your brand and engaging with customers. And if you're offering a service, apps like TaskRabbit or Fiverr can connect you with clients looking for exactly what you offer. The digital world is your playground—use it to your advantage.

2.6 Staying Ahead of the Curve

The hustle is constantly evolving, and so should you. The needs of your community will change, new technologies will emerge, and the market will shift. To stay ahead, you must be proactive in seeking out new opportunities and be willing to pivot when necessary.

Keep an eye on trends in your industry, stay informed about changes in your community, and always be on the lookout for the next big thing. This doesn't mean you should chase every new trend, but rather that you should be aware of what's happening and be ready to adapt if it aligns with your goals.

2.7 Execution: Moving from Idea to Action

Having a great idea is just the beginning. The real magic happens when you take that idea and turn it into a reality. This means creating a plan, setting goals, and executing with precision. Don't wait for the perfect moment—start small, test your idea, and refine it as you go. The sooner you start, the sooner you can begin learning, growing, and succeeding.

In this chapter, we've explored how to identify opportunities in the midst of struggle. By shifting your perspective, listening to your community, leveraging technology, and staying ahead of the curve, you can turn challenges into profitable ventures. The next step is to take those opportunities and run with them, turning your hustle into a thriving business. The hustle begins with identifying opportunities, but success comes from execution.

Chapter 3

Chapter 3: The Hustler's Mindset

Cultivating Resilience, Creativity, and Relentless Drive

The success of any entrepreneur starts with a mindset—a hustler's mindset. It's a mentality that refuses to accept failure as the final destination and embraces every challenge as an opportunity to grow. To succeed in the competitive world of business, especially in underserved communities, the hustler's mindset is essential. This chapter will take you through what it means to think like a hustler and how to cultivate the traits necessary to thrive, even when the odds seem stacked against you.

1. Resilience: Bouncing Back Stronger

Every entrepreneur faces setbacks, failures, and obstacles, but what separates a hustler from the rest is resilience. Resilience is your ability to recover quickly from difficult situations and adapt to changing circumstances. It's not about avoiding failure but using it as a tool to learn and improve. When things don't go as planned—and they often won't—you need to pick yourself up, dust off, and keep moving forward.

How to Build Resilience:

- **Embrace Failure as Feedback:** Understand that failure is not an endpoint but a lesson. Analyze what went wrong, adjust your approach, and try again.
- **Develop a Routine:** When things get tough, having a set routine can keep you grounded and focused. Whether it's exercising, meditating, or working in a specific environment, routines build stability in chaotic times.
- **Surround Yourself with Positivity:** The company you keep has a huge impact on your mindset. Surround yourself with people who encourage you to push through challenges rather than dwell on them.

2. Creativity: Solving Problems Differently

In entrepreneurship, creativity is more than just a skill—it's a necessity. Hustlers are natural problem-solvers who can look at the same situation as everyone else but see opportunities that others overlook. Whether it's developing new products, finding unconventional solutions to problems, or creating innovative marketing strategies, thinking creatively is key to staying ahead of the competition.

How to Boost Your Creativity:

- **Think Outside the Box:** Don't be afraid to approach problems from a different angle. Ask yourself, "What if I did the opposite of what everyone else is doing?" This can lead to breakthrough ideas.
- **Take Inspiration from Everywhere:** Creativity is often sparked by unexpected sources. Learn from other industries, cultures, or even nature. Sometimes, the best solutions come from places you never thought to look.
- **Stay Curious:** The most creative minds never stop asking questions. Be curious about how things work, why they fail, and how they can be improved. Curiosity fuels creativity.

3. Relentless Drive: The Engine of Success

The hustler's mindset is fueled by an insatiable hunger for success. It's the relentless drive to keep pushing, even when the road gets tough. Hustlers don't sit and wait for opportunities to fall into their laps—they go out and create them. This drive isn't about working hard aimlessly; it's about working smart with purpose and clarity.

How to Cultivate Relentless Drive:

- **Set Clear Goals:** Without clear, actionable goals, your energy can be wasted on unimportant tasks. Break your big dreams into smaller, manageable milestones and celebrate each win.
- **Stay Consistent:** Drive isn't about burning out by working 24/7; it's about consistently taking steps toward your goals. The more disciplined you are, the closer you get to your destination.
- **Embrace Competition:** Instead of shying away from competition, embrace it. Competition forces you to stay sharp and continuously improve your craft.

4. The Hustler's Mentality in Action

Let's look at some real-world examples of the hustler's mindset in action:

- **Jay-Z:** From growing up in the Marcy Projects of Brooklyn to becoming a billionaire mogul, Jay-Z exemplifies the hustler's mentality. His resilience allowed him to overcome adversity, his creativity helped him revolutionize music and business, and his relentless drive pushed him to venture into industries like fashion, sports management, and tech.

- **Sara Blakely:** Founder of Spanx, Blakely started with just $5,000 in savings and a single idea. She faced countless rejections but stayed creative, even cutting the feet out of pantyhose to demonstrate her product. Blakely's drive and ability to turn obstacles into opportunities led her to build a billion-dollar empire.
- **Nipsey Hussle:** Nipsey built his empire with the mindset of a hustler. From selling mixtapes out of his trunk to establishing a clothing store in South LA, he constantly gave back to the community and embraced innovative business strategies. His relentless drive and community-focused creativity inspired generations of entrepreneurs.

5. Building Your Hustler's Toolkit

To develop the hustler's mindset, you need to cultivate a toolkit of mental strategies:

- **Adaptability:** The ability to pivot when necessary and change course without getting discouraged is key. If one avenue isn't working, don't be afraid to shift to another.
- **Patience:** Hustlers know that success doesn't come overnight. The real hustle is a marathon, not a sprint.
- **Self-Awareness:** Know your strengths and weaknesses. Self-awareness allows you to hone your skills and delegate tasks you're less adept at to others.

6. Maintaining the Hustler's Mindset Long-Term

Once you've built the hustler's mindset, maintaining it is crucial. The journey doesn't end when you achieve your first success. Staying focused, adaptable, and driven as you grow your ventures is essential to long-term achievement.

- **Keep Evolving:** The business world is constantly changing, and you need to evolve with it. Stay ahead of trends and never stop learning.
- **Celebrate Your Wins:** Take time to celebrate your achievements, no matter how small. Celebrating boosts morale and gives you the energy to keep hustling.
- **Give Back:** The true mark of a hustler is one who gives back to the community that shaped them. Use your success to inspire and lift others.

The hustler's mindset is a combination of resilience, creativity, and relentless drive. It's the fire that keeps you going when the world tells you to quit. With this mindset, there is no obstacle too big, no failure too great, and no dream out of reach. Whether you're starting with nothing or building on existing success, the hustler's mindset will carry you to the next level.

Next Chapter: Now that you've developed the mindset, it's time to build your personal brand. In the next chapter, we'll dive into how to create a brand that not only reflects who you are but also stands out in a crowded market.

4

Chapter 4

Chapter 4: Building Your Personal Brand

Standing Out in a Crowded Market

In today's fast-paced and competitive business world, it's not enough to have a great product or service—you need a strong personal brand that distinguishes you from the rest. Your personal brand is more than a logo or a catchy tagline; it's the perception people have of you and the value you bring to the table. It reflects your mission, your hustle, and the story you're telling the world. In this chapter, we'll break down the steps to build a personal brand that resonates with your audience and sets you apart in the crowded marketplace.

1. Defining Your Brand Identity

The first step in building a personal brand is defining who you are and what you stand for. Your brand identity should be authentic to you, but it also needs to align with the goals of your business and the audience you want to attract.

Ask yourself the following questions to clarify your brand identity:

- **What's your mission?** What's the core purpose of what you do? This could be related to the problem you solve or the value you create for your customers.
- **What are your values?** Identify the principles that guide your business and how you interact with your audience. These values will define your brand's tone and how it's perceived.
- **What's your story?** Every successful brand has a compelling story that connects with people on an emotional level. Whether it's overcoming adversity or turning a passion into a business, your story is what makes you relatable and memorable.

By defining these aspects, you lay the foundation for a brand that's both genuine and impactful. Remember, authenticity is key. Trying to be something you're not will only distance you from your audience in the long run.

2. Establishing Your Unique Selling Proposition (USP)

To stand out, you need to define what makes you unique. Your **Unique Selling Proposition (USP)** is the factor that differentiates you from the competition and convinces potential customers or clients to choose you. It's not just about what you offer but about how and why you do it better than anyone else.

How to craft a powerful USP:

- **Highlight your strengths:** Focus on what you excel at. This could be your industry experience, a unique perspective, or a specialized service.
- **Solve a specific problem:** Identify the pain points of your target audience and clearly explain how you address them in a way no one else can.
- **Keep it concise:** Your USP should be easily communicated in a sentence or two. It should be straightforward and leave no doubt as to what makes you different.

3. Creating a Visual Identity

Your visual identity is how your brand presents itself to the world. It includes your logo, color schemes, typography, and overall design aesthetic. It's important because first impressions matter, and a cohesive visual identity helps your audience instantly recognize you.

Key elements of a strong visual identity:

- **Logo:** Your logo is the face of your brand. It should be simple, memorable, and reflective of your brand's values.
- **Colors and fonts:** The colors you choose can evoke specific emotions. For example, blue often represents trust, while red signals excitement or passion. Fonts also play a big role in setting the tone for your brand. Keep your colors and fonts consistent across all your branding materials.
- **Imagery:** Whether it's photos, illustrations, or videos, the imagery you use should resonate with your brand's story and mission. High-quality, professional visuals elevate your brand and create a lasting impression.

A strong visual identity is key to creating brand recognition. When people see your logo, colors, or style, they should immediately think of you and your business.

4. Crafting Your Personal Brand Message

Your personal brand message is what you communicate to your audience about who you are, what you do, and why it matters. It should be clear, concise, and consistent across all your platforms—whether you're speaking at an event, posting on social media, or networking in person.

Developing a compelling brand message involves:

- **Clear positioning:** Your message should explain the value you bring to the table and why you're the best at what you do.
- **Consistency:** Whether you're on social media, your website, or speaking in public, your brand message should be consistent. Repetition helps to cement your brand in people's minds.

- **Authenticity:** Be real in your messaging. People can spot inauthenticity a mile away, so make sure your brand message aligns with your true self and values.

Your brand message should create a connection with your audience, speaking to their needs and how you're uniquely positioned to meet them.

5. Establishing Your Online Presence

In the digital age, your online presence is crucial to building and sustaining your personal brand. Social media, a website, and other digital platforms allow you to showcase your brand and connect with a global audience. Establishing a strong and consistent online presence can help you engage with customers, share your story, and expand your reach.

Here's how to strengthen your online presence:

- **Create a website:** Your website is your digital business card. It's where people go to learn more about you, your story, and your services. Make sure it's professional, easy to navigate, and clearly communicates your brand message.
- **Leverage social media:** Platforms like Instagram, LinkedIn, Twitter, and Facebook allow you to engage directly with your audience. Choose platforms where your target market is most active, and post content that's relevant, valuable, and consistent with your brand.
- **Content marketing:** Position yourself as a thought leader in your industry by creating content that educates and informs your audience. Whether it's blog posts, videos, or podcasts, content marketing helps establish your expertise and reinforces your brand message.

Your online presence is where your audience gets to know you. Make sure it reflects your brand and is consistently updated with fresh content.

6. Building Trust and Credibility

Trust is one of the most valuable assets for any brand. You can have the best products or services, but without trust, customers won't engage with you. Credibility is built through authenticity, consistency, and delivering on promises. It takes time to build, but once earned, it becomes a powerful driver of growth.

How to build trust with your audience:

- **Show results:** Provide testimonials, case studies, or examples of your work to demonstrate the value you bring.
- **Be consistent:** Delivering on your brand's promises consistently is key to building credibility. Over time, people will trust that you can deliver what you say you will.
- **Engage transparently:** Transparency in communication builds trust. Whether you're sharing your business's challenges or successes, be honest with your audience.

7. Networking to Expand Your Brand

While your brand starts with you, expanding it relies on building relationships. Networking is a critical component of personal branding, as it allows you to connect with others who can help amplify your message. Whether it's in person at events or through digital platforms like LinkedIn, effective networking can lead to partnerships, referrals, and new opportunities.

Effective networking strategies include:

- **Be genuine:** When networking, focus on building real relationships, not just transactional exchanges. Take a genuine interest in others, and don't always look for what you can get out of the relationship.
- **Give value first:** Offer help, advice, or support to others before asking for something in return. Building goodwill will strengthen your network and open doors.
- **Follow up:** Networking doesn't end after the initial conversation. Be sure to follow up with new connections and maintain relationships over time.

8. Evolving and Maintaining Your Brand

Your personal brand isn't static. As you grow, so should your brand. Whether you're expanding into new industries, launching new products, or evolving your business model, it's important to regularly evaluate and refine your brand to stay relevant.

Steps to maintain and evolve your brand:

- **Regular self-assessment:** Periodically take a step back and assess whether your brand still reflects who you are and where you want to go.
- **Stay adaptable:** The market changes, and so should you. Stay ahead of trends and be willing to make adjustments when necessary.
- **Invest in your brand:** Continue learning and developing your skills to keep your brand strong. Take courses, attend conferences, and stay active in your industry.

Building a personal brand is a journey, not a one-time effort. It requires consistent action, self-awareness, and a willingness to evolve. By defining your identity, creating a strong message, establishing an online presence, and building trust with your audience, you can stand out in the crowded marketplace and create a brand that lasts.

Next Chapter: Now that your brand is set, it's time to master the financial side of your hustle. In the next chapter, we'll explore how to manage your money when traditional banking isn't an option and how to navigate the financial jungle of entrepreneurship.

5

Chapter 5

Chapter 5: Navigating the Financial Jungle

Managing Money When Traditional Banking Isn't an Option

In the world of entrepreneurship, managing your finances is one of the most important—and often most difficult—skills to master. For many of us, the traditional financial system just isn't built to support our hustle. Banks turn us down for loans, credit is hard to come by, and the idea of venture capital seems like a distant dream. But that doesn't mean we're out of the game. It just means we have to navigate the financial jungle on our own terms.

This chapter is about learning to play the financial game when the rules seem stacked against you. It's about finding creative ways to manage your money, make it work for you, and avoid the pitfalls that can derail your hustle. Whether you're bootstrapping your business or looking for alternative funding sources, this chapter will show you how to take control of your financial destiny.

1. Understanding the Financial Realities of Entrepreneurship

Before we dive into the strategies, let's start by facing the cold, hard truth: money is tight when you're starting out. You might not have access to traditional funding, and if you're coming from a community where financial resources are already scarce, it can feel like you're hustling just to stay afloat.

But here's the thing—most successful entrepreneurs started out exactly where you are now. They had to figure out how to make their money stretch, how to invest wisely, and how to navigate the financial hurdles in their way. It's not about having a big budget; it's about being smart with what you have.

Financial Hustle Tip:

Don't get discouraged by your current financial situation. Focus on the opportunities you have in front of you, and always keep in mind that small moves, when done consistently, can lead to big changes.

Real-Life Example:

Consider how small food vendors manage their money. They often start with very limited capital, yet they find ways to make it work—buying ingredients in bulk, sticking to cash-based sales, and gradually expanding as profits increase. They didn't wait for bank loans to build their business—they started with what they had and built from there.

2. Budgeting Like a Hustler

You can't manage what you don't track. One of the biggest mistakes entrepreneurs make is not keeping track of where their money is going. You need to be on top of every dollar that comes in and goes out. This means creating a budget that works for your hustle, even if it's lean.

A good budget isn't just about cutting costs—it's about making sure your money is working as hard as you are. A smart budget allows you to invest in growth, sustain operations, and weather financial storms.

Steps to Create a Hustler's Budget:

- **List Your Income Streams:** Whether it's your side hustle, main business, freelance gigs, or even rental income, write down all the ways money is coming into your pocket. Don't ignore the smaller streams—together, they can make a significant impact.
- **Track Every Expense:** Every coffee run, software subscription, and Uber ride counts. Use apps like **Mint** or **YNAB (You Need a Budget)** to categorize your expenses automatically. Break your spending down into personal and business expenses so you can easily identify where you might be overspending.
- **Cut Non-Essentials:** Take a hard look at what's not directly contributing to growth or essential operations. Cut back on unnecessary expenses like fancy office décor, high-end gadgets, or unnecessary software subscriptions until your cash flow improves.
- **Allocate Money for Growth:** Invest at least a small portion of your revenue back into areas that drive growth, such as marketing or equipment upgrades. Even if you have limited resources, prioritize spending that helps your hustle expand.

Detailed Tip:

Use the **50/30/20** rule for a balanced approach to budgeting:

- 50% of your income goes toward essentials (rent, utilities, necessary tools).
- 30% goes toward growth opportunities (marketing, professional development, etc.).
- 20% is saved or allocated to your emergency fund.

3. Managing Cash Flow: The Lifeblood of Your Hustle

Cash flow is the lifeblood of your business. No matter how great your product or service is, if you're not managing your cash flow, you'll struggle to keep your business running. The key is to make sure you always have enough cash on hand to cover your expenses while also reinvesting in growth.

Cash Flow Strategies for Hustlers:

- **Get Paid Faster:** One of the biggest cash flow killers is waiting too long to get paid. Set clear payment terms upfront, such as **net-15** or **net-30** (indicating when payment is due). Offer incentives for early payments or require deposits for larger projects.

- **Invoice Immediately:** Always send invoices as soon as the work is done, and make it easy for your clients to pay. Use online invoicing tools like **FreshBooks** or **QuickBooks** that send automatic payment reminders and allow you to accept credit card payments for faster transactions.
- **Negotiate with Vendors:** If you have relationships with vendors or suppliers, negotiate longer payment terms—such as **net-60**—so you have more time to collect payments from your customers before your bills are due.
- **Set Aside a Cash Reserve:** Even if money is tight, try to set aside a small emergency fund, aiming for at least 10-15% of your revenue. Having a financial cushion gives you peace of mind and the ability to handle unexpected expenses.

Detailed Example:

Imagine you run a small graphic design firm. You finish a large project but don't get paid for 60 days. Meanwhile, you still need to pay your rent, internet bill, and software subscriptions. By setting up net-30 terms with your clients and negotiating net-60 terms with your suppliers, you can cover your expenses while waiting for the client's payment, smoothing out your cash flow.

4. Building Credit When You Don't Have Access to Banks

If you've ever applied for a business loan, you know how hard it can be to get one—especially if you don't have stellar credit or a long financial history. But building credit is possible, even without the traditional banking system. And the truth is, good credit can be your ticket to bigger opportunities.

How to Build Credit as an Entrepreneur:

- **Start with a Secured Credit Card:** If your credit score is low or non-existent, a secured credit card is a good starting point. These cards require a deposit but help build your credit as long as you make on-time payments. Look for secured cards that report to all three major credit bureaus: **Equifax**, **Experian**, and **TransUnion**.
- **Use Alternative Lenders:** Online lending platforms like **Kiva**, **Lendio**, or **OnDeck** cater to small businesses with limited credit history. These lenders often have less strict criteria than traditional banks and can offer microloans to get you started.
- **Get Trade Credit:** Many vendors offer trade credit, allowing you to purchase goods and pay for them later, typically within 30 to 90 days. This helps establish a business credit history without requiring a traditional loan.
- **Register with Dun & Bradstreet:** Your **DUNS number** acts as a business identifier for potential lenders and creditors. Registering with Dun & Bradstreet helps you establish a business credit profile, which can increase your credibility and make you eligible for future financing.

Credit Building Hustle Tip:

Make sure every bill you have is paid on time, from utilities to trade credit accounts. Every missed or late payment sets you back, so consistency is key when building your credit profile.

5. Making Money Work for You: The Power of Investments

It's easy to fall into the mindset of working for every dollar. But if you want to take your hustle to the next level, you have to learn how to make your money work for you. Investing in your business—or even outside of it—can help you build wealth over time.

Where to Start with Investing:

- **Invest in Yourself First:** This includes education, certifications, or any resources that improve your skill set or business operations. For example, enrolling in a marketing course could dramatically increase your ability to promote your business and reach new clients.
- **Reinvest Profits into Your Business:** Whether it's buying more inventory, upgrading equipment, or hiring help, putting profits back into your business helps fuel growth. Invest in areas where you're seeing traction or need support.
- **Explore Small Investments:** If you have extra cash, consider putting small amounts into stocks, bonds, or even **crowdfunded real estate** through platforms like **Fundrise**. Start small and diversify to reduce risk while building your investment portfolio.

Investment Hustle Tip:

Be patient and strategic. Investing is about long-term growth, not quick returns. Even reinvesting in small but consistent ways can yield significant results over time.

6. The Art of Bartering: Trading Value When Cash is Tight

When money is tight, don't be afraid to get creative. Bartering—trading goods or services without exchanging money—can be a powerful way to get what you need without breaking your budget. Bartering allows you to preserve cash flow while still obtaining vital services or products.

Bartering Tips:

- **Offer Skills in Exchange for Services:** Think about the skills you have that are in demand. For instance, if you're a web designer, you could offer to redesign a local shop's website in exchange for catering or office supplies.
- **Build Partnerships:** Partner with businesses in complementary industries. For example, if you run a social media marketing business, you could offer free promotion for a photographer in exchange for professional headshots.
- **Negotiate Everywhere:** Don't be afraid to ask if a vendor is open to bartering. You might be surprised at how many people are willing to trade, especially if you offer something valuable in return.

Real-Life Example:

A personal trainer might offer discounted workout sessions to a local café in exchange for free or discounted meals. This not only reduces their personal expenses but also opens up cross-promotion opportunities for both businesses.

7. Avoiding Financial Pitfalls

In the hustle, it's easy to make mistakes with your money—especially when things are moving fast. But some financial pitfalls can cost you big if you're not careful. Learning to avoid these traps can save you from costly mistakes that derail your business.

Common Financial Pitfalls to Watch Out For:

- **Taking on Too Much Debt:** Borrowing money can be a necessary part of scaling your business, but it's a double-edged sword. Before taking on debt, consider whether you'll realistically be able to pay it back within the terms, and only borrow what you need to grow.
- **Failing to Separate Business and Personal Finances:** Mixing your business and personal finances can cause confusion, tax issues, and limit your ability to track profits and losses. Open a separate bank account for your business and always keep finances distinct.
- **Not Paying Yourself:** In the early stages, it's tempting to reinvest everything into the business, but don't forget to pay yourself a salary. Even if it's small, consistent pay keeps you motivated and prevents financial burnout.

Avoiding Pitfalls Hustle Tip:

Make reviewing your finances a weekly habit. Track your expenses, check your income, and adjust your budget regularly to avoid falling into bad financial habits.

Mastering the financial side of your hustle takes time, patience, and a lot of grit. But once you learn how to navigate the financial jungle, you'll not only survive—you'll thrive. Whether you're bootstrapping, building credit, or learning to invest, the strategies in this chapter will help you turn every dollar into an opportunity.

Next Chapter: Now that you've got a handle on your finances, it's time to focus on building relationships that will fuel your hustle. In the next chapter, we'll dive into the art of networking and how to leverage connections to grow your business.

6

Chapter 6

Chapter 6: Mastering the Art of Networking

Leveraging Connections for Business Growth

No matter how hard you hustle, one truth remains: success in business isn't just about what you know—it's about who you know. Networking is the art of building relationships that will propel your hustle forward. Whether you're just starting out or scaling your business, connections open doors that talent alone can't. From mentors and investors to partners and customers, the people you know can help you grow faster, smarter, and stronger.

Pause for a second and ask yourself:

Who's in my network right now?

Do I have mentors who guide me? Partners who share my vision? Customers who are loyal and excited about my brand?

If you're missing some key players, don't worry—that's what this chapter is about. You're going to learn how to network like a hustler: with purpose, authenticity, and hustle. You'll connect with the right people, build relationships that matter, and leverage those connections to grow your business.

Let's get into it.

1. The Power of Relationships in Business

Before we dive into strategies, it's important to understand why networking is essential. At its core, business is about people. Every deal, collaboration, investment, and opportunity is built on relationships. The stronger your relationships, the more likely you are to succeed.

In underserved communities, networking is even more critical because opportunities are often harder to come by. When resources are limited, relationships become the bridges to success. Your network can connect you to the capital, knowledge, and partnerships you need to break through.

Ask Yourself:

- *Who do I know that has access to opportunities I need?*
- *How can I build relationships with people who are outside of my immediate circle?*

Think about it. Every business deal is a handshake away. The question is, whose hand are you shaking?

Why Relationships Matter in Business:

- **Access to Opportunities:** Networking opens doors to opportunities you might not otherwise find. A single introduction can lead to a big contract, new customer, or key investor.
- **Mentorship and Guidance:** Having experienced people in your corner can help you avoid costly mistakes. Mentors offer advice, insights, and lessons learned from their own experiences.
- **Building Trust:** Business is built on trust, and trust is built through relationships. When people know and trust you, they're more likely to do business with you or refer you to others.

Action Step:

Take 5 minutes to write down the names of 5 people who could help you unlock a new opportunity. If you can't think of anyone, that's your first signal: it's time to expand your network.

2. Networking with Purpose

Let's be real: not all networking is created equal. It's not about how many people you know; it's about knowing the right people. Networking without purpose is like fishing in a puddle—you won't catch anything. You need to be intentional, focusing on building connections that align with your goals and hustle.

Ask Yourself:

What's my goal when I network?

Are you looking for potential customers? Mentors? Investors? Partnerships? Your goal will shape how you approach networking and the kind of people you want to meet.

Steps to Network with Purpose:

- **Define Your Goals:** Before attending an event or reaching out to someone, be clear on what you're trying to achieve. If you're looking to grow your business, seek out potential customers or partners. If you need advice, focus on finding mentors.
- **Identify Key Players:** Who are the decision-makers, influencers, and gatekeepers in your industry or community? Do your research—know who holds the keys to the opportunities you want and who can connect you to them.
- **Be Strategic with Your Time:** Not all networking opportunities are worth your time. Choose events and gatherings where your ideal connections will be, whether that's industry conferences, local business meetups, or online communities.

Networking Hustle Tip:

It's not about collecting business cards or followers—it's about creating **meaningful** relationships. Focus on quality over quantity.

Action Step:

Write down your top 3 networking goals for the next 6 months. Who do you want to connect with? How will this help your hustle?

3. Making a Memorable First Impression

Let's keep it real: your first impression can make or break a potential connection. Whether it's at a networking event or a casual introduction, how you present yourself in those first few moments sets the tone for the relationship. Think about it—if you've only got a few seconds to make an impression, you better make it count.

How to Make a Strong First Impression:

- **Be Authentic:** People can spot fake from a mile away, so be yourself. Authenticity is key to building trust and lasting relationships. Let your passion for your hustle shine through.
- **Have Your Elevator Pitch Ready:** You need to be able to explain who you are, what you do, and why it matters in 30 seconds or less. Make your pitch compelling but concise. The goal is to pique interest, not overwhelm them with details.
- **Show Interest in Others:** A lot of people think networking is about selling themselves, but the truth is—people love to talk about themselves. Ask questions, listen actively, and engage. People remember those who take the time to listen.

Elevator Pitch Example:

"I run a small digital marketing agency that helps local businesses build their online presence and grow their customer base. In fact, I recently helped a restaurant increase their revenue by 30% in just 3 months through targeted social media campaigns. I'd love to learn more about your business."

Action Step:

Practice your elevator pitch right now. Time yourself. Can you explain your business in 30 seconds or less? If not, refine it.

4. Building Relationships That Last

Okay, you've made a great first impression. Now what? The real magic happens **after** the first meeting. Building long-term, meaningful relationships requires time, effort, and consistency. Networking isn't about one-off meetings—it's about cultivating relationships that matter.

How to Build Strong Relationships:

- **Follow Up:** After meeting someone, don't let too much time pass before you follow up. Send a personalized message thanking them for their time and referencing something specific from your conversation. This shows you were paying attention.
- **Offer Value First:** One of the biggest mistakes people make is asking for something too soon. Instead, think about how you can offer value to the other person first. This could be advice, a resource, or an introduction to someone in your network. Giving before you ask builds goodwill.

- **Stay Consistent:** Don't let months pass before you reconnect with someone. Relationships require nurturing. Stay in touch, share updates, or simply check in regularly to see how they're doing.

Networking Hustle Tip:

The strongest relationships are built on mutual benefit. Always ask yourself, "What can I offer this person before I ask for something?"

Action Step:

Identify 3 people in your network that you haven't followed up with in a while. Reach out today. Send a quick email or text to check in.

5. Leveraging Digital Networking

In today's world, networking isn't just about face-to-face meetings. Platforms like LinkedIn, Twitter, and industry-specific forums offer incredible opportunities to connect with people all over the world. You don't have to be in the same room to make a powerful connection.

Ask Yourself:

- *Is my online presence strong enough to attract the right connections?*
- *Am I engaging with others in my industry online, or am I just a spectator?*

Digital Networking Strategies:

- **Optimize Your Profiles:** Whether you're on LinkedIn or Twitter, make sure your profiles reflect who you are and what you do. Use professional photos, write a compelling bio, and highlight key accomplishments.
- **Engage with Purpose:** Don't just post content—interact with others. Comment on posts, share insights, and engage in conversations. Your goal is to become part of the community, not just an observer.
- **Join Online Communities:** Whether it's LinkedIn groups, Reddit threads, or niche forums, find spaces where people in your industry gather and start engaging. These communities are often goldmines for advice, partnerships, and opportunities.

Action Step:

Take 10 minutes today to review your LinkedIn profile. Does it clearly communicate your brand? If not, update it to reflect who you are and what you offer.

6. Turning Contacts into Collaborators

Networking isn't just about collecting contacts—it's about turning those contacts into collaborators. These are the people who will actively help you grow your hustle, whether it's through partnerships, joint ventures, or mentorship. The goal is to find win-win situations where both sides benefit.

How to Turn Contacts into Collaborators:

- **Identify Mutual Goals:** Successful collaborations are built on aligned goals. What do you and the other person hope to achieve, and how can you help each other get there?
- **Be Clear About Expectations:** Set clear expectations from the start. Make sure both sides understand what they're bringing to the table and what the desired outcome is.
- **Maintain Open Communication:** Keep communication open throughout the collaboration. Check in regularly to make sure things are on track and that both parties are satisfied.

Action Step:

Think of one person in your network you could collaborate with. Reach out and propose a small, low-risk project you could work on together.

7. Expanding Your Network Beyond Your Comfort Zone

Here's where most people get stuck—they network only with people like themselves. The real growth happens when you step outside your comfort zone and connect with people from different backgrounds, industries, and perspectives. Some of the best opportunities come from unexpected places.

Expanding Your Network:

- **Network Across Industries:** Don't limit yourself to your industry. Some of the best collaborations happen when people from different fields bring new ideas together.
- **Diversify Your Contacts:** Surround yourself with people from different walks of life. The more diverse your network, the more unique insights and opportunities you'll uncover.
- **Attend Unconventional Events:** Go to events that aren't directly related to your industry. Whether it's a community event or a creative workshop, you never know who you'll meet.

Action Step:

Find an event or community outside your usual circles and commit to attending this month. Your next big opportunity could come from a place you least expect.

8. The Long Game: Building a Network That Supports Your Legacy

Here's the thing—networking is about playing the long game. The relationships you build today will shape your future. Whether you're looking for business opportunities, mentorship, or lifelong collaborators, the people you connect with will play a key role in building your legacy.

How to Build a Long-Term Network:

- **Invest in Your Network:** Like any good relationship, networking takes time and effort. Don't be the person who only reaches out when they need something. Invest in your relationships consistently.
- **Give More Than You Take:** The most successful networkers are givers. When you focus on providing value to others, people naturally want to support you in return.

- **Build a Reputation of Trust:** Your reputation is everything. Always act with integrity, follow through on your promises, and be known as someone who can be trusted. A solid reputation will open more doors than any pitch ever could.

Action Step:

Reflect on how you've invested in your network this year. Could you give more? Could you reach out more often? Make a commitment to nurture those relationships consistently.

Conclusion:

Mastering the art of networking is a game-changer for any hustler. The relationships you build will open doors, provide guidance, and create opportunities that money alone can't buy. Approach networking with authenticity, purpose, and patience, and you'll find yourself surrounded by a powerful network of people who are just as invested in your success as you are.

Next Chapter: Now that you've mastered the art of networking, it's time to tackle the pivot. In the next chapter, we'll explore how to adapt and shift strategies when the game changes, and how to turn setbacks into comebacks.

7

Chapter 7

Chapter 7: The Art of the Pivot

Adapting and Shifting Strategies to Overcome Obstacles

No business journey is a straight path to success. Every entrepreneur, no matter how well-prepared, will face unexpected challenges that demand flexibility and resilience. The ability to pivot—changing direction when the original plan isn't working—is a critical skill for any hustler. It's the difference between giving up when things get tough and finding a new way to win. Whether it's shifting your business model, adjusting your target market, or exploring new revenue streams, mastering the art of the pivot is essential to staying in the game.

Pause and reflect:

Is there something in your business that's not working?

Is your growth slower than expected? Are you constantly running into the same obstacles?

In this chapter, we'll explore when, why, and how to pivot. You'll learn how to recognize when it's time to change course, the steps to take when pivoting your business, and how to turn obstacles into opportunities. And we'll dive deep into the real-world examples of companies who've pivoted successfully, showing you that your next big win could be just one strategic change away.

1. Recognizing When It's Time to Pivot

Pivoting doesn't mean abandoning your hustle—it means being smart enough to recognize when something isn't working and bold enough to try something new. But how do you know when it's time to pivot versus sticking it out and pushing harder?

Here are some signs that it might be time to change direction:

- **Stagnant Growth:** If your business is consistently hitting a wall and you're not seeing the growth you expected, it could be a sign that your current approach isn't resonating with your audience.
- **Changing Market Conditions:** The market is constantly evolving. If consumer behavior, industry trends, or technology shifts in a way that makes your current business model less relevant, it's time to adapt.

- **Consistent Negative Feedback:** If your customers are telling you the same thing over and over—whether it's about your product, service, or pricing—you need to listen. Negative feedback is often a sign that something needs to change.
- **Burnout:** If you're losing passion for your hustle, feeling constantly overwhelmed, or burning out, it could be a sign that your current direction isn't sustainable.

Recognizing these signs early can save you time, money, and energy. The key is to pivot before you hit rock bottom—not after.

Ask Yourself:

Am I holding onto a failing strategy because I'm afraid to change?

Is there another path I haven't explored yet that could lead to greater success?

Action Step:

Take 10 minutes to reflect on your current business strategy. Write down 3 things that are working and 3 things that aren't. Do you see any patterns that suggest it's time to pivot?

2. The Mental Shift: Embracing Change

Pivoting is never easy. It requires you to let go of what you thought would work and open yourself up to new possibilities. This mental shift can be difficult, especially when you've invested a lot of time, money, and effort into a particular strategy. But hustlers know that clinging to a failing plan is a recipe for disaster.

How to Embrace the Pivot:

- **Detach Emotionally from Your Original Idea:** It's easy to become emotionally attached to the plan you started with. But in business, emotional attachment can cloud your judgment. Take a step back and evaluate your business objectively. Is your current strategy really working, or are you holding onto it because it's familiar?
- **Focus on the Bigger Picture:** A pivot isn't a failure—it's an adjustment on your path to success. Keep your long-term vision in mind and remember that the road to success is rarely a straight line. Every pivot is a step closer to finding the right formula for your hustle.
- **Stay Open to New Opportunities:** Sometimes, the best opportunities come from unexpected places. Stay curious, keep learning, and be willing to explore new ideas—even if they take you in a different direction than you originally planned.

Ask Yourself:

What's holding me back from embracing change?

Am I holding onto an old plan because I'm afraid of starting over?

Remember: change isn't failure—it's progress.

Action Step:

Write down one part of your business where you feel stuck. Now, brainstorm at least 3 new directions you could explore to get things moving again. Don't be afraid to think outside the box.

3. Types of Pivots

Not all pivots look the same. Depending on your business and the challenges you're facing, you may need to pivot in different ways. Here are some common types of pivots that entrepreneurs make:

- **Product Pivot:** This involves changing your product or service offering to better meet the needs of your customers. Maybe your original product isn't solving the problem you thought it would, or there's a new opportunity in the market that you hadn't considered. A product pivot might mean adding new features, redesigning your product, or launching a completely new offering.
- **Market Pivot:** Sometimes, your product is solid, but you're targeting the wrong audience. A market pivot involves shifting your focus to a different customer base. This could mean targeting a different demographic, geographic location, or industry.
- **Revenue Model Pivot:** If your current pricing or revenue model isn't generating enough income, it might be time to change how you make money. This could mean switching from a one-time purchase model to a subscription model, introducing new pricing tiers, or finding alternative revenue streams like licensing or partnerships.
- **Technology Pivot:** In some cases, new technology emerges that can help you deliver your product or service more effectively. A technology pivot involves adopting new tools, platforms, or processes to improve your operations and stay competitive.

Pivoting Hustle Tip:

Don't feel like you need to pivot everything at once. Focus on the area that's causing the most friction in your business and make adjustments there first.

Action Step:

Identify one area of your business where a pivot could make a significant difference. Is it your product, market, or revenue model? Outline what this pivot would look like in practical terms.

4. Steps to Execute a Successful Pivot

Once you've recognized the need to pivot, it's time to take action. Pivoting requires a clear plan, execution, and communication to ensure a smooth transition. Here are the steps to execute a successful pivot:

1. **Assess Your Current Situation:** Before making any changes, take a deep dive into your business to understand what's not working and why. Analyze your sales data, customer feedback, market trends, and financials. This will help you identify the root cause of your challenges.

2. **Identify the Pivot Opportunity:** Based on your assessment, decide what kind of pivot is necessary. Is it a product change, a market shift, or a new revenue model? Be clear about the opportunity you're pursuing and why it makes sense for your business.
3. **Test the Waters:** Don't pivot blindly. Before fully committing to the new direction, test your ideas with a small group of customers or in a limited market. This will allow you to gather feedback and validate your new approach without risking everything.
4. **Communicate the Change:** Whether you're pivoting internally or externally, it's important to communicate the change clearly to all stakeholders. This includes your team, customers, investors, and partners. Explain why you're pivoting, how it will improve your business, and what they can expect moving forward.
5. **Implement the Pivot:** Once you've validated your new direction, it's time to fully implement the pivot. This might involve rebranding, updating your website, launching a new product, or reaching out to a new customer base. Stay focused, stay organized, and ensure that everyone on your team is aligned with the new strategy.
6. **Monitor and Adjust:** A pivot isn't a one-and-done move. After implementing your pivot, continue to monitor your results and be prepared to make additional adjustments as needed. Stay flexible and responsive to feedback so that you can fine-tune your new approach over time.

Action Step:

If you're considering a pivot, outline a small-scale test. How can you test your new idea with limited risk before fully committing?

5. Turning Setbacks into Comebacks

One of the biggest challenges entrepreneurs face when pivoting is the fear of failure. But here's the truth: every successful entrepreneur has faced setbacks. What separates the winners from the losers is how they respond to those setbacks. Instead of seeing them as roadblocks, hustlers see setbacks as opportunities to learn, grow, and come back stronger.

How to Turn a Setback into a Comeback:

- **Reflect on the Lessons:** Every setback has a lesson hidden in it. Whether it's a failed product launch or a lost client, take the time to reflect on what went wrong and what you can do differently next time.
- **Stay Resilient:** Pivoting takes courage, but it also requires resilience. There will be challenges along the way, but every challenge is an opportunity to strengthen your business and sharpen your skills. Stay focused on your end goal, and don't let temporary setbacks derail your vision.
- **Keep Moving Forward:** The most important thing after a pivot is to keep moving forward. Don't get stuck in analysis paralysis or second-guess your decision. Once you've committed to a new direction, give it your all and stay the course.

Ask Yourself:

How can I turn this setback into a lesson? What did it teach me about my business or approach?

Action Step:

Take one recent setback and write down what you learned from it. How will you apply those lessons moving forward?

6. Real-World Examples of Successful Pivots

Some of the most successful businesses in the world were built on pivots. Here are a few real-world examples of entrepreneurs who made strategic pivots that transformed their companies:

Slack: From Failed Gaming Company to Billion-Dollar Communication Platform

Slack is now one of the most widely used workplace communication tools in the world, but it didn't start out that way. The company originally launched as **Tiny Speck**, a gaming company behind an online game called *Glitch*. Despite a loyal fanbase, *Glitch* failed to gain widespread popularity, and after four years of development, Tiny Speck decided to shut the game down.

However, during the development of the game, the team at Tiny Speck had created an internal communication tool to help them work more effectively. After shutting down the game, they realized that this tool might have broader appeal, especially for teams looking to streamline their communication. They pivoted away from gaming and focused entirely on refining and marketing this internal messaging system—which became **Slack**.

Key Pivot Elements:

- **Product Pivot:** Tiny Speck shifted from being a gaming company to a software company, turning an internal tool into a new product.
- **Market Shift:** They moved from targeting gamers to targeting businesses that needed better communication tools.
- **Resilience:** The founders didn't view the failure of *Glitch* as the end. Instead, they found an opportunity in their setbacks and used it to pivot successfully.

Lesson:

The very tool you create to solve internal problems may be the next big thing for others. Don't be afraid to pivot if your core product doesn't take off; look at the solutions you've developed along the way.

Twitter: From Podcasting to Microblogging

Believe it or not, Twitter didn't start out as the global social media giant we know today. Originally, the company was called **Odeo**, and it was a platform designed to allow users to search for and subscribe to podcasts. However, in 2005, Apple launched **iTunes**, which included podcasting features. The Odeo team realized that they couldn't compete with Apple, and they quickly needed to find a new direction.

During a brainstorming session, one of the team members, Jack Dorsey, proposed a short messaging system that allowed users to send brief status updates to groups of people. This idea resonated, and Odeo pivoted from podcasting to microblogging, eventually launching **Twitter** in 2006.

Key Pivot Elements:

- **Complete Product and Market Pivot:** Odeo completely abandoned its original product and market, shifting from podcasting to creating a whole new category with microblogging.
- **Speedy Decision-Making:** The team quickly recognized they couldn't compete with Apple and acted decisively to pivot rather than trying to cling to a failing idea.
- **User-Driven Concept:** The idea for Twitter came from the team's internal brainstorming, and the simple concept of sharing short messages filled a gap no one knew existed.

Lesson:

Don't be afraid to let go of your original product, especially if a giant competitor enters the space. Sometimes, the pivot leads to something completely different—and much bigger.

Netflix: From DVD Rentals to Streaming Giant

When Netflix first launched in 1997, it was a DVD rental service that allowed customers to rent DVDs by mail. The company's unique subscription model quickly gained traction, and they built a loyal customer base. But by the mid-2000s, it was clear that the future of entertainment was shifting from physical media to digital. Rather than doubling down on their DVD rental service, Netflix made the bold decision to pivot to streaming, even though the technology wasn't widely available at the time.

In 2007, Netflix launched its streaming service, allowing subscribers to watch movies and TV shows online. It was a risky move, but it paid off. Today, Netflix is a global powerhouse, not only as a streaming platform but as a content creator producing some of the world's most popular original shows and movies.

Key Pivot Elements:

- **Business Model Pivot:** Netflix moved from a DVD rental business to a streaming service, anticipating the shift in consumer behavior before it became mainstream.
- **Long-Term Vision:** Instead of waiting for the market to fully shift, Netflix took the lead in developing a streaming service, betting that the future was digital.
- **Product Evolution:** Over time, Netflix didn't just stick to streaming other companies' content. They evolved to create original content, which has since become a major differentiator.

Lesson:

Being ahead of the curve is risky but can lead to massive success. Netflix saw where the future was headed and took action before competitors could catch up.

YouTube: From Dating Site to Video-Sharing Platform

It's hard to imagine YouTube as anything other than the video-sharing giant it is today, but it actually started out as a dating website. When it launched in 2005, **YouTube's** founders envisioned a site where people could upload video profiles and connect with potential romantic partners. However, they soon realized that users weren't interested in uploading videos for dating.

What they did notice, though, was that people were eager to upload and share all kinds of videos, not just dating profiles. The founders quickly pivoted from a niche dating site to a broader platform that allowed users to upload, share, and watch videos of any kind. This pivot transformed YouTube into the global video-sharing platform that would eventually be acquired by Google for $1.65 billion.

Key Pivot Elements:

- **User Behavior Insights:** The founders of YouTube noticed how users were using their platform in unexpected ways and pivoted to accommodate what users actually wanted.
- **Rapid Adaptation:** Rather than sticking to the original concept of a dating site, YouTube's founders were quick to shift their focus to a more promising opportunity.
- **Product Flexibility:** YouTube's pivot was a testament to how listening to users and adapting to their behavior can open up entirely new markets.

Lesson:

Your users will often show you the way. Pay attention to how customers are using your product, even if it's not the way you intended. The opportunity to pivot might be hidden in their actions.

Shopify: From Snowboard Equipment to E-Commerce Platform

Shopify is now synonymous with e-commerce, powering over 1 million online stores around the world. But the company wasn't always focused on helping businesses sell online. In fact, **Shopify** began as a company selling snowboard equipment online. When the founders, Tobias Lütke and Scott Lake, were unhappy with the available e-commerce platforms, they decided to build their own software to sell their snowboards.

As they worked on their online store, they realized that the platform they were developing was far more valuable than their original business of selling snowboards. Recognizing this opportunity, they pivoted from selling snowboards to offering an e-commerce platform that allowed anyone to create an online store. Shopify was born and has since become one of the leading e-commerce platforms in the world.

Key Pivot Elements:

- **From Product to Platform Pivot:** Shopify moved from selling a product (snowboards) to providing a service (e-commerce platform) that could be used by millions of businesses.
- **Solving Your Own Problem:** The founders created Shopify to solve their own problem, then realized that many other businesses needed the same solution.

- **Long-Term Focus:** Shopify's pivot wasn't just about creating a platform—it was about enabling entrepreneurship, a mission that has propelled its success.

Lesson:

Sometimes the solution you create for yourself is the one the world needs. If you're solving a problem for your own business, there's a good chance other businesses need the same solution.

PayPal: From Cryptography to Payments

PayPal started out as a company focused on cryptography and security software for handheld devices. But the team behind **PayPal** noticed that one particular feature of their platform—the ability to send money electronically—was getting more traction than anything else. They pivoted to focus entirely on electronic payments, which was a growing need in the early 2000s as e-commerce began to take off.

The shift paid off. PayPal became the go-to service for online payments, eventually being acquired by eBay for $1.5 billion in 2002. Today, PayPal is a household name in online transactions and continues to be a leader in the digital payment space.

Key Pivot Elements:

- **Feature-Based Pivot:** PayPal noticed that one feature of their platform was gaining more traction than the rest, so they pivoted to focus solely on that.
- **Riding the E-Commerce Wave:** The pivot happened at a time when e-commerce was still in its early stages, positioning PayPal as a key player in the future of online payments.
- **Scalable Model:** By focusing on payments, PayPal created a service that could scale globally, impacting millions of businesses and consumers.

Lesson:

Sometimes the most valuable part of your product isn't the one you expected. Keep an eye on what features your customers are using most—it could lead to your next pivot.

The stories of Slack, Twitter, Netflix, YouTube, Shopify, and PayPal demonstrate the power of the pivot. Whether you're adjusting your product, shifting your target market, or completely overhauling your business model, the ability to pivot is what keeps your hustle alive. Each of these companies faced challenges, but instead of giving up, they adapted and found new paths to success.

Action Step:

Reflect on your own business. Are there opportunities for a pivot that could lead to your next big breakthrough? What lessons can you take from these real-world examples to guide your own strategic shifts?

Next Chapter: Now that you've mastered the pivot, it's time to explore how to bootstrap your business and grow with limited resources. In the next chapter, we'll dive into creative strategies for building your empire without breaking the bank.

8

Chapter 8

Chapter 8: Bootstrapping Your Business

Growing with Limited Resources

Bootstrapping isn't just a buzzword in the entrepreneurial world—it's a reality for most hustlers. When access to capital is limited, or investors aren't an option, entrepreneurs must learn how to build their business from the ground up using the resources they already have. This means being scrappy, resourceful, and smart with your money. The good news? Some of the world's most successful companies were built by bootstrapping.

In this chapter, we'll cover how to grow your business when your funds are tight. You'll learn creative strategies for getting things done with minimal resources, how to reinvest profits wisely, and why starting small can often lead to bigger success. Bootstrapping isn't just about survival—it's about thriving on your own terms.

1. The Bootstrapping Mindset

Bootstrapping isn't just about managing finances—it's a mentality. It requires you to think differently about how you build your business, relying on creativity and resourcefulness rather than big budgets. Hustlers who master the art of bootstrapping understand that they don't need all the bells and whistles to succeed. Instead, they focus on maximizing the resources they have and being strategic about growth.

How to Develop a Bootstrapping Mindset:

- **Start with What You Have:** You may not have access to large amounts of capital, but you do have skills, relationships, and knowledge. Leverage those assets as much as possible.
- **Embrace Limitations as Opportunities:** Constraints force you to think creatively. When you don't have money to throw at problems, you're forced to find innovative solutions. This creativity often leads to stronger, more sustainable businesses.
- **Be Relentlessly Resourceful:** Bootstrapping requires you to make things happen, even when it seems like the odds are against you. This could mean bartering, negotiating better deals, or finding free tools to get the job done.

Bootstrapping Hustle Tip:

It's not about what you don't have—it's about how you use what you do have. Every limitation is an opportunity to think outside the box.

2. Starting Small and Growing Steadily

One of the biggest mistakes new entrepreneurs make is trying to grow too fast, too soon. When you're bootstrapping, it's essential to start small and focus on sustainable growth. Scaling too quickly without the resources to support it can lead to cash flow issues, burnout, and even failure.

Strategies for Starting Small:

- **MVP (Minimum Viable Product):** Don't wait until you have the "perfect" product or service to launch. Start with a Minimum Viable Product (MVP)—the simplest version of your offering that solves a problem for your customers. You can always improve and iterate as you grow.
- **Focus on Core Offerings:** Instead of trying to be everything to everyone, focus on doing one thing really well. Offering too many products or services can dilute your brand and stretch your resources too thin.
- **Reinvest Profits:** As you start making money, reinvest those profits back into your business. This could mean upgrading equipment, expanding your product line, or investing in marketing to reach new customers. Every dollar you make should have a clear purpose in growing your business.

3. Leveraging Free and Low-Cost Tools

Thanks to technology, there are countless free or low-cost tools available to help you run your business efficiently. From project management and marketing to accounting and customer service, there's no shortage of affordable resources that can save you time and money.

Essential Free or Low-Cost Tools:

- **Project Management:** Tools like Trello, Asana, and Monday.com offer free plans that help you stay organized, manage tasks, and collaborate with your team.
- **Marketing:** Canva is a free tool for creating social media graphics, presentations, and other visual content. Mailchimp offers free email marketing services for small lists, making it easy to stay connected with your audience.
- **Accounting:** Wave Accounting is a free platform for invoicing, tracking expenses, and managing your cash flow. It's ideal for entrepreneurs who don't have the budget for expensive accounting software.
- **Customer Service:** Google Forms or Typeform can be used to gather customer feedback or conduct surveys for free, helping you improve your products and services based on real insights.

Bootstrapping Hustle Tip:

Before paying for any service or tool, always check if there's a free version that meets your needs. Free tools can be surprisingly powerful when used effectively.

4. Bartering: Trading Value When Cash is Tight

When you're bootstrapping, cash can be scarce, but that doesn't mean you're out of options. Bartering—trading goods or services without exchanging money—is a powerful way to get what you need without spending cash. Whether it's exchanging marketing help for web design, or offering consulting services in exchange for equipment, bartering allows you to build your business without breaking the bank.

How to Make Bartering Work for You:

- **Identify What You Can Offer:** What services, skills, or products do you have that others might need? Whether it's marketing, web development, accounting, or even photography, you likely have something valuable to trade.
- **Find the Right Partners:** Look for other small businesses or freelancers who might need what you offer. Reach out through your network, attend local business events, or join online groups where entrepreneurs exchange services.
- **Negotiate Fairly:** Make sure both parties feel they're getting equal value in the exchange. Be clear about expectations, deadlines, and deliverables to avoid misunderstandings.

5. Building a Network to Support Your Growth

When you don't have access to big investors or loans, your network becomes one of your most valuable assets. From mentors and advisors to fellow entrepreneurs and customers, the relationships you build can provide the support, advice, and even resources you need to grow your business.

Ways to Build and Leverage Your Network:

- **Mentorship:** Seek out mentors who have experience in your industry. They can provide guidance on how to navigate challenges, avoid pitfalls, and grow your business strategically.
- **Partnerships:** Collaborate with other businesses that complement yours. For example, if you're a graphic designer, you could partner with a copywriter to offer joint services to clients.
- **Word of Mouth:** When you're bootstrapping, marketing dollars are limited. One of the best ways to promote your business is through word of mouth. Deliver exceptional value to your customers, and they'll spread the word for you.

6. Creative Revenue Streams

When you're bootstrapping, finding ways to generate revenue early and consistently is key. This often means thinking creatively about how to make money, even if it's outside your original business plan. Multiple revenue streams can help stabilize your cash flow and give you the resources you need to grow.

Ideas for Creative Revenue Streams:

- **Offer Consulting or Freelance Services:** If you have expertise in a specific area, consider offering consulting or freelance services as a way to generate extra income. This can help fund your business while you're still building your main product or service.
- **Pre-Sell Products or Services:** If you haven't fully developed your product yet, you can still generate revenue by pre-selling it. This means customers pay upfront for a product or service they'll receive later. It's a great way to raise funds without taking on debt.
- **Host Workshops or Events:** Hosting paid workshops, webinars, or events can help you generate additional revenue while also positioning you as an expert in your field.

7. Scaling Slowly but Strategically

Bootstrapping doesn't mean you can't scale—it just means you need to scale smart. Instead of going for rapid, unsustainable growth, focus on scaling your business one step at a time. This allows you to stay in control, avoid unnecessary risks, and keep your business lean.

How to Scale Strategically:

- **Prioritize High-Impact Activities:** When you're ready to grow, focus on the activities that will have the biggest impact. This could mean investing in marketing to reach more customers, improving your product to increase customer retention, or expanding your team to take on more work.
- **Automate Where Possible:** As you grow, look for ways to automate repetitive tasks. This could mean using email automation for marketing, setting up automated billing systems, or using software to manage inventory. Automation saves time and reduces errors.
- **Know When to Outsource:** When your business reaches a point where you're overwhelmed with tasks, consider outsourcing work that isn't your core strength. Hiring freelancers for things like accounting, web design, or social media management can free up your time to focus on growth.

8. The Power of Patience

Bootstrapping requires patience. Unlike businesses that receive large investments and can grow quickly, bootstrapped businesses often grow at a slower, steadier pace. While this might seem frustrating at times, remember that slow growth is often more sustainable in the long run. You have control over your business, your decisions, and your direction.

Why Patience Pays Off:

- **You Stay in Control:** When you're not relying on outside investors, you have full control over your business. This means you can grow at your own pace and make decisions that align with your vision.

- **You Build a Solid Foundation:** Bootstrapping forces you to build a strong foundation for your business. You'll learn how to manage your finances, make smart decisions, and grow sustainably—all of which lead to long-term success.
- **You Appreciate Every Win:** When you've built something from scratch, every win feels more meaningful. You'll appreciate the journey, and the success will be that much sweeter because you earned it through hard work and grit.

Bootstrapping is a hustle. It's about building something from nothing and turning limited resources into unlimited potential. While the journey might be slower, the rewards are greater. By starting small, staying resourceful, and scaling strategically, you'll build a business that stands the test of time—on your terms.

Next Chapter: Now that you've learned how to bootstrap your business, it's time to explore creative ways to secure funding. In the next chapter, we'll dive into unconventional funding sources, from microloans and crowdfunding to alternative capital options.

9

Chapter 9

Chapter 9: Securing Funding in Unconventional Ways

Exploring Microloans, Crowdfunding, and Alternative Capital Sources

Every entrepreneur faces the challenge of funding their business at some point, especially when bootstrapping can only take you so far. Traditional funding options—like bank loans, venture capital, or angel investors—aren't always available to everyone, particularly those from underserved communities. However, this doesn't mean you're out of options. In today's world, there are numerous unconventional ways to secure the capital you need to grow your business.

This chapter is about getting creative with your funding. We'll explore alternative sources of capital like microloans, crowdfunding, and other innovative approaches to financing. Whether you're launching your first side hustle or scaling your business, these strategies can help you secure the money you need without relying on traditional financial institutions.

1. Understanding the Power of Unconventional Funding

Before diving into specific options, it's important to understand why unconventional funding is so powerful. These alternative funding sources offer flexibility, accessibility, and, in many cases, they allow you to maintain control of your business without giving up equity or taking on massive debt.

Unconventional funding options often have lower barriers to entry, making them ideal for entrepreneurs in underserved communities who may not have access to traditional capital sources. They also allow you to leverage your community, customer base, and network to raise money in creative ways.

Why Unconventional Funding Works:

- **Lower Risk:** Many alternative funding options don't require you to risk personal assets or take on significant debt.
- **Community-Driven:** Crowdfunding and community-based loans allow you to build a network of supporters who are invested in your success.
- **Flexible Terms:** Unlike traditional loans, many of these options come with more flexible repayment schedules or investment structures.

Ask Yourself:

What funding options am I overlooking that could open new doors for my business?

2. Microloans: Small Loans, Big Impact

Microloans are small loans designed to help entrepreneurs who may not qualify for traditional financing. They are typically provided by nonprofit organizations, community-based lenders, or government programs, and they often come with lower interest rates and more flexible terms than traditional bank loans.

How Microloans Work:

- **Loan Amounts:** Microloans typically range from $500 to $50,000, making them ideal for businesses that need a small amount of capital to get started or to scale up.
- **Eligibility:** Microloans are often available to entrepreneurs who may not qualify for traditional bank loans due to lack of credit history, collateral, or limited financial resources.
- **Lenders:** Organizations like the **Small Business Administration (SBA)** in the U.S., **Kiva**, and **Accion** provide microloans to small businesses and startups.

How to Secure a Microloan:

1. **Research Lenders:** Look for microloan providers that specialize in your region, industry, or community. Each lender will have its own eligibility requirements, so be sure to review them carefully.
2. **Prepare a Solid Business Plan:** Even for small loans, lenders will want to see a clear business plan that outlines how you plan to use the funds and how you'll repay the loan.
3. **Build a Strong Application:** Highlight your unique strengths as an entrepreneur and how the loan will help you grow your business. Microloan providers often prioritize businesses with a strong community focus or social impact.

Action Step:

Research two microloan providers that align with your business goals and evaluate their application requirements.

3. Crowdfunding: Rallying Your Community for Support

Crowdfunding has become one of the most popular ways for entrepreneurs to raise money without giving up equity or taking on debt. By leveraging platforms like **Kickstarter**, **Indiegogo**, or **GoFundMe**, you can ask your community, customers, and supporters to contribute small amounts of money to fund your project or business.

Types of Crowdfunding:

- **Reward-Based Crowdfunding:** In exchange for contributions, you offer backers a reward—usually a product or service related to your business. This model is common on platforms like Kickstarter and Indiegogo.
- **Equity Crowdfunding:** With this model, backers invest in your business in exchange for equity. Platforms like **SeedInvest** or **WeFunder** facilitate this type of funding, but it typically requires more regulatory compliance.
- **Donation-Based Crowdfunding:** This type is ideal for community-focused or charitable businesses. Platforms like GoFundMe allow people to contribute without expecting anything in return.

How to Launch a Successful Crowdfunding Campaign:

1. **Set Clear Goals:** Determine exactly how much money you need to raise and what you'll use it for. Be transparent with your backers about how the funds will be spent.
2. **Tell a Compelling Story:** Your crowdfunding campaign is as much about your story as it is about your business. Share your journey, your vision, and why people should support your hustle.
3. **Offer Attractive Rewards:** If you're using reward-based crowdfunding, offer perks that entice backers to contribute. Whether it's early access to your product, exclusive merchandise, or special experiences, make sure your rewards are valuable.
4. **Leverage Your Network:** Start by reaching out to your existing community—friends, family, and social media followers. The first few contributions are crucial to building momentum and attracting more backers.

Crowdfunding Hustle Tip:

Crowdfunding isn't just about raising money—it's also a marketing tool. Use your campaign to generate buzz and build a community of loyal supporters around your brand.

Action Step:

If you're considering a crowdfunding campaign, start by outlining the story behind your business. What makes your story compelling enough for people to want to invest in your journey?

4. Peer-to-Peer Lending: Borrowing from Your Network

Peer-to-peer (P2P) lending platforms like **LendingClub**, **Prosper**, or **Funding Circle** connect entrepreneurs directly with individual investors who are willing to lend money. These platforms eliminate the need for traditional banks and often come with more flexible terms.

How P2P Lending Works:

- **Application Process:** You submit a loan request on a P2P lending platform, outlining how much you need, your business plan, and how you'll repay the loan.

- **Investors Review Your Request:** Individual investors browse loan requests and decide whether to fund all or part of your loan. Each investor contributes a portion of the total loan amount.
- **Repayment:** Like a traditional loan, you'll make regular payments (including interest) to the investors who funded your loan.

Pros of P2P Lending:

- **More Accessible:** P2P lending often has less stringent credit requirements than traditional banks, making it easier for entrepreneurs with limited credit histories to secure funding.
- **Flexible Terms:** Many platforms offer flexible repayment terms and interest rates that are often lower than those of traditional lenders.

How to Succeed with P2P Lending:

- **Be Transparent:** Provide detailed information about your business, financials, and how you plan to use the loan. Transparency builds trust with potential lenders.
- **Highlight Your Strengths:** Investors are more likely to lend to businesses with strong potential for growth. Emphasize your experience, market opportunity, and any traction you've gained so far.

5. Angel Investors in Underserved Communities

Angel investors are individuals who invest their own money in early-stage businesses in exchange for equity. While this might sound similar to venture capital, angel investors are often more flexible and willing to take risks on startups with limited resources. They're especially valuable for entrepreneurs in underserved communities because they provide both capital and mentorship.

Finding Angel Investors:

- **Local Angel Groups:** Many cities have angel investor groups that meet regularly to hear pitches from local entrepreneurs. Research groups in your area, such as **Tech Coast Angels** in California or **Golden Seeds** for women-led ventures.
- **Online Platforms:** Platforms like **AngelList** or **Gust** allow you to connect with angel investors who are interested in specific industries or regions.
- **Networking Events:** Attend events, conferences, and pitch competitions where angel investors are likely to be present. Building relationships with investors in person can increase your chances of securing funding.

Angel Investor Hustle Tip:

Angel investors are often looking for more than just a great idea—they want to invest in passionate, resilient entrepreneurs. Be sure to convey your dedication, vision, and long-term goals when pitching to an angel.

Action Step:

Research local or online angel investor groups that align with your industry. Start preparing your pitch by highlighting what makes you and your business unique.

6. Government Grants and Competitions

In many countries, government programs offer grants, competitions, and funding opportunities for small businesses, particularly those owned by women, minorities, or entrepreneurs in underserved communities. Unlike loans, grants don't need to be repaid, making them an attractive option for entrepreneurs with limited resources.

Examples of Grant Programs:

- **Small Business Innovation Research (SBIR):** A U.S. government program that provides grants to small businesses engaged in innovative research and development.
- **Amber Grant:** This grant is specifically for women entrepreneurs and awards $10,000 each month to a female-owned business.
- **Local Business Development Programs:** Many cities and states have business development programs that offer grants or low-interest loans to support local entrepreneurs.

How to Secure a Grant:

1. **Research Available Grants:** Look for grant programs that align with your industry, business size, and location. Many grants have specific eligibility criteria.
2. **Prepare a Strong Application:** Grant applications often require a detailed business plan, financial projections, and a clear explanation of how you'll use the funds. Make sure your application is thorough and professional.
3. **Demonstrate Impact:** Many grant programs prioritize businesses that create jobs, have a social impact, or benefit underserved communities. Highlight how your business contributes to these areas.

Securing funding doesn't always have to follow the traditional route of bank loans or investors. With microloans, crowdfunding, peer-to-peer lending, angel investors, and government grants, you have a wide array of options to fuel your business's growth. The key is to be creative, persistent, and open to new ways of raising capital.

Next Chapter: Now that you know how to secure funding, it's time to focus on leveraging technology to grow your business. In the next chapter, we'll dive into the digital tools and strategies that can help you scale your hustle, even on a limited budget. From social media marketing to automation, you'll learn how to maximize the power of technology to reach more customers and streamline your operations.

10

Chapter 10

Chapter 10: Digital Hustle: Leveraging Technology

U*sing Apps, Social Media, and Online Platforms to Enhance Your Business*

In the modern world, technology is a hustler's best friend. It's the great equalizer, leveling the playing field for entrepreneurs who may not have access to traditional resources. Whether you're running your business from your phone, marketing on social media, or using online platforms to reach customers around the globe, the right technology can take your hustle to the next level.

In this chapter, we'll explore how to leverage technology to enhance your business, streamline your operations, and expand your reach. From using social media to build a brand, to tapping into digital platforms that automate your tasks, we'll cover the tools and strategies that will help you work smarter, not harder.

1. Building Your Brand on Social Media

Social media is one of the most powerful tools for any entrepreneur. It allows you to connect directly with your audience, build your brand, and promote your products or services—all without spending a dime. Whether you're on Instagram, Facebook, TikTok, or LinkedIn, your social media presence can be a game-changer for your business.

How to Build a Strong Social Media Presence:

- **Choose the Right Platforms:** You don't need to be on every social media platform. Focus on the ones where your target audience is most active. For visual brands, Instagram and TikTok might be best. For B2B businesses, LinkedIn is a strong option.
- **Create Engaging Content:** Post content that adds value to your audience, whether it's educational, entertaining, or inspirational. Use a mix of photos, videos, and stories to keep your audience engaged. Show behind-the-scenes footage, share customer testimonials, and use your posts to tell your story.
- **Stay Consistent:** Consistency is key to growing your following. Post regularly and engage with your audience by responding to comments and messages. You don't need to post daily, but aim for consistency so your audience knows when to expect new content.

- **Use Hashtags and Tags:** Hashtags help increase your visibility and can attract new followers who are interested in your niche. Use popular hashtags in your industry, but also create your own branded hashtags to build a community around your brand.

Social Media Hustle Tip:

Don't just focus on selling—build a relationship with your audience. Share your journey, struggles, and wins. People are more likely to support brands they feel connected to on a personal level.

2. Automating Your Business with Apps and Tools

Running a business is a lot of work, but with the right technology, you can automate many of your tasks and free up time to focus on growth. From managing customer relationships to tracking expenses, there are apps and platforms that handle it all. Automating your business allows you to work smarter and scale faster.

Essential Tools for Automation:

- **Customer Relationship Management (CRM):** Tools like **HubSpot** or **Zoho CRM** help you manage customer interactions, track leads, and automate follow-ups.
- **Email Marketing:** Platforms like **Mailchimp** or **Constant Contact** automate your email marketing campaigns, from sending welcome emails to nurturing leads with targeted content.
- **Scheduling Tools:** If you manage appointments, tools like **Acuity Scheduling** or **Calendly** can automate the booking process, making it easy for clients to schedule meetings or services without back-and-forth emails.
- **Accounting and Invoicing:** Tools like **QuickBooks** or **FreshBooks** help you automate invoicing, expense tracking, and financial reporting, ensuring that you stay on top of your finances with minimal effort.

Automation Hustle Tip:

Start small—automate one part of your business at a time. Identify the most repetitive tasks and find tools to streamline them. Gradually, you'll free up more time to focus on high-impact areas of your business.

3. Leveraging E-Commerce Platforms

If you're selling products or services, having an online store is essential. E-commerce platforms make it easy for you to reach a global audience, manage sales, and grow your business without needing a physical storefront.

Popular E-Commerce Platforms:

- **Shopify:** One of the most popular e-commerce platforms, Shopify allows you to set up an online store quickly, manage inventory, process payments, and market your products. It's ideal for entrepreneurs who want a user-friendly platform that scales with their business.

- **Etsy:** If you're selling handmade or unique items, Etsy provides a built-in audience of customers looking for creative, artisanal products. It's perfect for small businesses looking to tap into a niche market.
- **Amazon Marketplace:** Selling on Amazon gives you access to millions of potential customers. It's great for scaling your business quickly, but keep in mind that competition is fierce, and Amazon takes a significant percentage of your sales.
- **Wix or Squarespace:** These platforms allow you to create custom websites with integrated e-commerce features. They're perfect for entrepreneurs who want more control over their website design and branding.

E-Commerce Hustle Tip:

Don't just rely on one sales channel. If possible, sell through multiple platforms to reach different customer segments. For example, you could have your main store on Shopify while also selling on Amazon and Etsy.

4. Building an Online Community

Building a loyal customer base is key to growing a successful business, and one of the best ways to do this is by creating an online community. Whether it's a Facebook group, a Slack community, or a Discord server, an online community allows you to engage with your customers on a deeper level, get feedback, and turn them into brand advocates.

Steps to Build an Online Community:

- **Choose the Right Platform:** Decide where you want to host your community. Facebook groups are great for reaching a broad audience, while platforms like Slack or Discord are ideal for more niche, engaged groups.
- **Provide Value:** Your community should offer more than just product promotions. Share valuable content, host Q&A sessions, offer exclusive deals, and give your members a reason to keep coming back.
- **Encourage Engagement:** Ask questions, start discussions, and encourage your members to share their experiences with your brand. The more engaged your community is, the more loyal they'll become.
- **Be Active:** Communities thrive when the founder or brand leader is actively involved. Respond to questions, share updates, and participate in discussions regularly.

Community Hustle Tip:

Your community can be one of your most valuable assets. Treat your members with respect, show appreciation for their support, and make them feel like a vital part of your brand.

5. Digital Marketing: Reaching a Global Audience

In the digital age, your business is no longer limited by geography. With digital marketing, you can reach customers around the world from the comfort of your home. Whether it's through social media advertising, search engine optimization (SEO), or pay-per-click (PPC) ads, digital marketing gives you the power to scale your business quickly and efficiently.

Key Digital Marketing Strategies:

- **SEO:** Search engine optimization helps your website rank higher on search engines like Google. By optimizing your site for relevant keywords, you can attract more organic traffic without paying for ads.
- **PPC Advertising:** Platforms like Google Ads and Facebook Ads allow you to target specific audiences with paid ads. You can set a budget, create targeted campaigns, and track your performance in real-time.
- **Content Marketing:** Content is king in the digital world. By creating high-quality blog posts, videos, or podcasts that provide value to your audience, you can build trust, improve your SEO, and attract more customers.
- **Social Media Advertising:** Platforms like Instagram and Facebook allow you to run targeted ads based on demographics, interests, and behaviors. Social media advertising is one of the most cost-effective ways to reach a large audience.

Digital Marketing Hustle Tip:

Experiment with different marketing strategies and track your results. What works for one business might not work for another, so it's important to test and optimize your approach.

6. Staying Connected with Remote Tools

As your business grows, you may need to collaborate with a team, partners, or freelancers. Thanks to remote tools, you can stay connected and manage your business efficiently from anywhere in the world.

Popular Remote Tools:

- **Zoom:** Ideal for virtual meetings and webinars, Zoom allows you to connect with team members, clients, or customers in real-time.
- **Slack:** Slack is a powerful communication tool for teams. It allows you to create different channels for specific topics, share files, and integrate other tools like Google Drive or Trello.
- **Google Workspace:** Google Workspace (formerly G Suite) provides everything you need for remote collaboration, including email, cloud storage, and document sharing.

Remote Work Hustle Tip:

Even if you're running a solo operation, staying organized and using remote tools can help you scale efficiently as you grow your business.

7. Expanding Your Business Internationally

One of the biggest advantages of the digital age is the ability to expand your business internationally. With online platforms, you can sell your products or services to customers in different countries without ever leaving your home.

Steps to Go Global:

- **International Shipping:** If you're selling physical products, research international shipping options and costs. Platforms like **ShipStation** or **Easyship** can help you manage international orders efficiently.
- **Currency and Payment Processing:** Ensure your e-commerce platform supports multiple currencies and payment methods. Services like **PayPal**, **Stripe**, or **Shopify Payments** make it easy to accept payments from customers around the world.
- **Localization:** To connect with customers in different countries, consider localizing your website and marketing materials. This might involve translating your content, adapting your messaging to fit cultural norms, and offering local payment options.

Global Hustle Tip:

Start by targeting one or two international markets before expanding further. Focus on countries where there is demand for your products or services, and build from there.

Technology isn't just a tool—it's a catalyst for growth. By embracing digital platforms, automation tools, and online marketing strategies, you can scale your business, reach a global audience, and create a brand that thrives in the digital age. Whether you're running a small side hustle or building a full-fledged empire, technology will play a critical role in your success.

Next Chapter: Now that you've harnessed the power of technology, it's time to build your team. In the next chapter, we'll dive into how to assemble the right people to support your vision and help take your business to the next level.

Chapter 11

Chapter 11: Building a Solid Team

Assembling the Right People to Support Your Vision

No matter how talented or determined you are, success in business is never achieved alone. To truly scale your hustle and turn your vision into reality, you need a team that shares your drive and complements your strengths. Building a solid team is about more than hiring employees—it's about surrounding yourself with people who believe in your mission, bring diverse perspectives, and are committed to helping your business grow.

In this chapter, we'll explore the steps to assembling the right people to support your vision, from identifying key roles to fostering a culture of trust and collaboration. Whether you're looking to bring on your first hire, partner with freelancers, or expand to a full-fledged team, getting the right people in place can propel your business to new heights.

1. The Power of a Strong Team

The bigger your business grows, the more you'll realize that no entrepreneur can succeed in isolation. As your workload increases and your goals become more ambitious, the only way to keep up is by leveraging the strengths of others. A solid team amplifies your capabilities, allowing you to delegate tasks, scale more efficiently, and tap into diverse skills that drive innovation and growth.

Why a Strong Team is Crucial:

- **Increased Efficiency:** You can't do everything alone. A good team enables you to focus on high-level strategy while delegating specialized tasks to others.
- **Diverse Perspectives:** When you bring together people with different backgrounds, experiences, and skills, you open your business up to fresh ideas and innovative solutions.
- **Sustainable Growth:** Scaling your business requires more than just hard work—it requires smart systems and people who can handle the demands of growth without overwhelming you or diluting the quality of your work.

Team-Building Hustle Tip:

Don't wait until you're completely swamped to start building your team. If you hire when you're already overwhelmed, you risk rushing the process. Start small with freelancers or part-timers to handle the tasks that pull you away from your core strengths.

2. Identifying the Key Roles for Your Business

Before you start hiring, it's essential to identify the specific roles that will have the most impact on your business. Start by analyzing your workload and pinpointing where you're spending too much time or where you lack expertise. Then, prioritize the roles that can free up your time and strengthen the areas of your business where you need support.

Key Roles to Consider:

- **Operations Manager:** Handles the day-to-day processes that keep your business running, including logistics, inventory management, scheduling, and quality control. This person ensures that your business operates smoothly behind the scenes.
- **Marketing and Sales Specialist:** Whether you need help managing social media, running paid ads, or closing deals, a marketing or sales expert can grow your audience, drive revenue, and increase brand awareness.
- **Financial Advisor or Accountant:** As your business grows, managing cash flow, budgeting, and taxes becomes more complex. A financial expert helps you stay on top of your finances and make informed decisions to maintain profitability.
- **Customer Support:** Maintaining strong relationships with your customers is critical to long-term success. A dedicated customer support specialist ensures that inquiries, complaints, and feedback are handled promptly and professionally.
- **Product or Service Lead:** Whether you're selling a product or delivering a service, this person focuses on ensuring quality, innovation, and continuous improvement. They oversee the development and refinement of your offerings to meet customer needs.

Freelancers vs. Full-Time Employees:

When you're just starting to build your team, you may not need full-time staff for every role. Freelancers or part-time employees can fill specialized roles (like content creation or graphic design) while keeping costs low and providing flexibility.

3. Finding the Right People

Building a successful team is about finding the right people who align with your vision and culture. It's not just about hiring someone who can do the job—it's about finding individuals who are passionate about your mission and willing to go the extra mile to help your business grow.

Where to Find Talent:

- **Referrals and Your Network:** One of the most reliable ways to find great talent is through referrals. Ask your network, mentors, and fellow entrepreneurs for recommendations—they often know qualified individuals who would be a great fit.
- **Freelance Platforms:** Sites like **Upwork**, **Fiverr**, or **Toptal** provide access to freelancers with a wide range of skills, allowing you to hire for specific tasks or short-term projects without committing to full-time employment.
- **Job Boards and Social Media:** Platforms like **LinkedIn**, **Indeed**, and **AngelList** are excellent for posting job openings and connecting with potential candidates. Social media can also be a powerful tool to attract talent, especially if your brand already has a strong presence.
- **Internship Programs:** Interns bring fresh perspectives and enthusiasm to your business. While they may lack experience, they often make up for it with passion and eagerness to learn. If they're a good fit, interns can eventually transition into full-time employees.

Hiring Hustle Tip:

When hiring, prioritize values, work ethic, and cultural fit over technical skills. Skills can be taught, but drive, passion, and alignment with your company's mission are qualities that are harder to find and harder to instill.

4. Creating a Collaborative Culture

Once you have the right people in place, it's essential to create a culture of collaboration, trust, and shared vision. A strong team culture motivates employees to bring their best selves to work every day, fosters creativity, and leads to better overall performance.

How to Build a Collaborative Team Culture:

- **Communicate Your Vision:** Make sure every team member understands the mission and vision of your business. When people feel connected to a shared purpose, they're more likely to put in the extra effort and stay motivated.
- **Encourage Open Communication:** Foster an environment where team members feel comfortable sharing their ideas, providing feedback, and asking questions. Regular check-ins, open-door policies, and team meetings ensure that everyone stays aligned.
- **Promote Collaboration Across Departments:** Break down silos and encourage teamwork between different departments or roles. When people collaborate and share insights, they can come up with better solutions to challenges.
- **Celebrate Wins:** Recognize both big achievements and small milestones. Whether it's a shout-out in a meeting, a bonus, or simply acknowledging someone's hard work, celebrating wins builds morale and strengthens your team's commitment to the business.

Culture Hustle Tip:

As the leader, you set the tone for your company's culture. Lead by example—whether that's through transparency, accountability, or showing appreciation for your team's efforts.

5. Motivating and Retaining Top Talent

Building a great team is only half the battle—keeping them engaged and committed is just as important. Retaining top talent requires more than just paying competitive salaries; it's about creating an environment where people feel valued, supported, and challenged.

Strategies to Motivate and Retain Your Team:

- **Opportunities for Growth:** High-performing employees want to know they have room to grow. Offer opportunities for career advancement, mentorship, and professional development to keep them engaged and motivated.
- **Empowerment:** Give your team members the autonomy to make decisions and take ownership of their work. When people feel empowered and trusted, they're more likely to take initiative and perform at a high level.
- **Recognize and Reward Achievements:** Regularly acknowledge hard work and successes. This could be through bonuses, additional vacation days, or simply public recognition during team meetings. People stay loyal when they feel appreciated.
- **Promote Work-Life Balance:** Burnout is real, and it can hurt your team's productivity and well-being. Encourage a healthy work-life balance by offering flexible work hours, remote work options, or mental health support.

Retention Hustle Tip:

Retaining great talent is about creating a work environment where people feel they are making a meaningful contribution. Invest in your team's development and well-being, and they'll invest in your business's success.

6. Knowing When to Let Someone Go

Not every hire will be a perfect fit, and holding onto the wrong person can hurt your business in the long run. Recognizing when it's time to let someone go is a difficult but necessary part of building a strong team.

How to Handle Letting Go:

- **Evaluate Performance Early:** If a team member isn't meeting expectations, address the issue as soon as possible. Be clear about your expectations and offer constructive feedback. If performance doesn't improve after several conversations, it may be time to part ways.
- **Be Direct and Compassionate:** Letting someone go is never easy, but it's important to handle it with respect. Be clear about the reasons for the decision and offer support where appropriate.

- **Learn from the Process:** Reflect on whether there were any red flags during the hiring process or onboarding. Use this experience to improve how you evaluate and onboard new hires in the future.

Letting Go Hustle Tip:

It's always better to address performance issues early. Keeping someone who isn't contributing can create resentment among your other team members and hinder the progress of your business.

7. Scaling Your Team as You Grow

As your business expands, so will your team. Scaling your team strategically is essential to managing growth without losing the quality of your product or services.

How to Scale Your Team:

- **Plan for Growth:** Identify the key milestones that will require additional hires, such as expanding into new markets, launching new products, or hitting certain revenue goals. Have a plan in place for when and how you'll bring on new team members.
- **Delegate Responsibilities:** As your team grows, you'll need to delegate authority to managers or department heads. This allows you to focus on big-picture strategy while others handle day-to-day operations.
- **Maintain Company Culture:** Rapid growth can dilute your company culture if you're not careful. Make sure every new hire understands and aligns with your business's values to maintain the strong culture you've built.

Scaling Hustle Tip:

Take your time when scaling your team. Growing too fast can lead to misaligned hires, communication breakdowns, and cultural disconnects. Be intentional with every new addition to your team.

Building a strong, cohesive team is one of the most important investments you can make in your business. Surrounding yourself with people who share your passion, bring diverse perspectives, and are dedicated to your mission allows you to scale, innovate, and succeed at a higher level. Whether it's finding your first hire or expanding into a larger team, focus on building relationships with individuals who complement your strengths and enhance your business's potential.

Next Chapter: Now that you've built a strong team, it's time to market your hustle without breaking the bank. In the next chapter, we'll explore budget-friendly marketing strategies to get the word out and grow your customer base creatively and effectively.

Chapter 12

Chapter 12: Hustling in Multiple Industries

Balancing and Succeeding in Diverse Ventures

Entrepreneurship is often seen as a single-track journey, where success comes from focusing on one venture at a time. But for many hustlers, the true art lies in balancing multiple businesses across different industries. Whether you're running a tech startup, managing a retail brand, or investing in real estate, hustling across industries can be a powerful way to diversify income, mitigate risks, and expand your influence.

In this chapter, we'll dive deep into how to manage and excel in multiple ventures without spreading yourself too thin. You'll learn strategies for balancing priorities, leveraging your strengths, and creating synergy between different businesses. When done right, hustling in multiple industries can lead to greater financial security and more opportunities for long-term success.

1. The Benefits of Hustling Across Multiple Industries

Running multiple businesses comes with its own set of challenges, but the benefits of diversification can outweigh the complexities. By branching out into different industries, you're positioning yourself to withstand market fluctuations, tap into new opportunities, and cross-pollinate ideas from one sector to another.

Why Hustling in Multiple Industries is a Smart Move:

- **Diversified Income Streams:** If one industry hits a rough patch, the other ventures can keep you afloat. Diversifying reduces the financial risks associated with putting all your eggs in one basket.
- **Cross-Industry Learning:** Different industries come with different challenges and innovations. The lessons you learn in one industry—like customer service strategies or marketing tactics—can often be applied to another, leading to innovative solutions and fresh perspectives.
- **Expanded Network and Influence:** Each industry introduces you to a new set of contacts, clients, and collaborators. By engaging in multiple sectors, you can build a larger, more varied network, increasing opportunities for partnerships and growth.

Multi-Industry Hustle Tip:

Look for synergies between your ventures. You don't have to operate in silos. The experience, knowledge, and resources from one industry can often benefit the others, making you more efficient and effective overall.

2. Mastering Time Management: The Key to Balancing Multiple Ventures

When you're running businesses across industries, time management becomes your greatest asset. With so many moving parts, it's easy to become overwhelmed. Success lies in knowing how to prioritize, delegate, and streamline your efforts so each venture receives the attention it needs.

How to Balance Multiple Ventures:

- **Set Priorities Based on Immediate Needs:** Each business will have different demands at different times. Some days, one venture will require more of your attention due to a product launch or a key partnership. Prioritize your businesses based on their immediate needs and long-term potential.
- **Use a Structured Schedule:** Block specific times for each business. Whether it's dedicating a few hours a day to one venture or assigning specific days of the week, structure helps prevent constant switching between businesses, which can lead to inefficiency.
- **Delegate Tasks to Trusted Teams:** As your businesses grow, you won't be able to handle everything alone. Build teams you trust and delegate daily operations so you can focus on big-picture strategy and growth for each venture.

Time Management Hustle Tip:

Batch similar tasks across ventures. For example, handle all your marketing efforts for multiple businesses in one go rather than bouncing between marketing, operations, and product development for different companies.

3. Leveraging Your Strengths Across Different Industries

One of the greatest advantages of running businesses in multiple industries is the ability to leverage your core strengths across each venture. Whether it's your expertise in sales, leadership, or marketing, the skills you've honed in one industry can be applied to other businesses, increasing your impact.

How to Leverage Your Strengths Across Ventures:

- **Identify Your Core Competencies:** Reflect on your top skills—whether it's managing people, developing products, or closing deals. Use these skills to fuel your efforts in every venture you manage.
- **Develop Repeatable Processes:** Once you've found a successful process in one business—like customer acquisition or managing inventory—apply that same approach to your other ventures. Standardizing operations across businesses saves time and improves efficiency.

- **Build a Strong Personal Brand:** Your personal brand can create credibility across multiple industries. By positioning yourself as an expert in one field, you can use that influence to gain attention and trust in other sectors. This can also lead to opportunities for cross-promotion between ventures.

Strengths Hustle Tip:

Don't shy away from borrowing ideas from one industry and applying them to another. Sometimes the most innovative solutions come from mixing strategies across completely unrelated sectors.

4. Creating Synergy Between Your Ventures

The most successful multi-industry entrepreneurs create synergy between their businesses. By aligning your ventures in complementary ways, you can amplify growth, share resources, and generate more value across the board.

Ways to Create Synergy Between Ventures:

- **Cross-Promotion:** Use your different businesses to promote one another. For example, if you run a marketing agency and a retail brand, use the agency's skills to drive sales for your retail business, while offering marketing services to other retailers.
- **Shared Resources:** Pool resources where possible. This could include sharing an office space, using the same accounting or payroll software, or centralizing administrative tasks. Shared resources reduce costs and streamline operations.
- **Collaborative Ventures:** Look for ways to create joint ventures between your businesses. If you run a consulting firm and an events company, consider hosting conferences or events that showcase your consulting expertise while promoting your events business.

Synergy Hustle Tip:

Always think about how one venture can support the other. Whether through clients, services, or resources, creating synergy between your businesses allows you to scale faster with fewer resources.

5. Managing Risk Across Multiple Ventures

While diversifying your entrepreneurial portfolio can protect you from market fluctuations, it also introduces new risks. Managing multiple businesses means managing different sets of risks—financial, operational, and market-related. To succeed, you need a strategy for balancing these risks.

How to Manage Risk:

- **Diversify Your Ventures:** Ensure that your ventures are not overly reliant on the same market or economic conditions. For example, running both a retail business and a tech company protects you if one industry faces a downturn.

- **Monitor Cash Flow:** Keep close tabs on the financial health of each business. Avoid using funds from one venture to support another unless it's a calculated move. Maintain separate budgets and track performance individually.
- **Be Flexible and Ready to Pivot:** If one business isn't performing as expected, don't be afraid to pivot or refocus. Part of managing multiple ventures is knowing when to shift your efforts to the businesses that show the most promise at any given time.

Risk Management Hustle Tip:

Don't overextend yourself. Maintain a financial buffer for each business to handle unexpected challenges without putting your other ventures at risk.

6. Staying Focused Amidst Competing Priorities

Running multiple ventures requires laser focus to avoid distractions and stay productive. With so many competing priorities, it's easy to get overwhelmed or lose track of what matters most. Developing strategies to stay focused and organized is essential to your success.

How to Stay Focused:

- **Limit Distractions:** Identify your biggest distractions, whether it's constant email notifications or unnecessary meetings, and minimize them. Set boundaries for your workday to ensure uninterrupted focus.
- **Set Clear Goals for Each Business:** Define specific, measurable goals for each venture. These goals will guide your actions and ensure that every decision is aligned with moving your businesses forward.
- **Use Productivity Tools:** Leverage tools like **Trello**, **Asana**, or **Notion** to track tasks, manage projects, and stay organized. These platforms allow you to visualize your priorities and keep everything running smoothly across your ventures.

Focus Hustle Tip:

Work on one business at a time. Instead of multitasking, dedicate focused time to each venture and complete tasks fully before switching to the next. This approach will help you maintain momentum and avoid burnout.

7. Knowing When to Scale Back

Hustling across multiple industries is rewarding, but it's also demanding. There may come a time when you need to scale back to preserve your energy, mental health, or resources. Recognizing when to scale back is critical to maintaining your long-term success.

Signs It's Time to Scale Back:

- **Burnout:** If you're feeling overwhelmed, fatigued, or disconnected from your businesses, it may be time to pause and reassess. Overextending yourself can lead to poor decision-making and diminish the quality of your work.
- **Underperforming Ventures:** If one business is consistently underperforming and draining resources, it may be worth considering whether to continue investing in it or to focus your energy on your more profitable ventures.
- **Lack of Focus:** If managing multiple ventures is causing you to lose focus on your core strengths or the ventures with the highest potential, scaling back may allow you to regain clarity and drive better results.

Scaling Back Hustle Tip:

Scaling back doesn't mean giving up—it's about being strategic with your time and energy. Prioritizing your strongest ventures can ultimately lead to greater success and a more sustainable workload.

Hustling in multiple industries is a bold and rewarding path, offering a range of opportunities to diversify income, create synergy, and tap into new markets. By effectively managing your time, leveraging your strengths, and staying focused, you can succeed across diverse ventures without losing your balance. The key is to stay adaptable, avoid burnout, and know when to scale back or pivot when necessary.

Next Chapter: Now that you've learned how to balance multiple industries, it's time to explore creative ways to market your businesses on a budget. In the next chapter, we'll dive into cost-effective marketing strategies that will help you get the word out and grow your customer base.

Chapter 13

Chapter 13: Marketing on a Budget

Creative and Cost-Effective Strategies for Getting the Word Out

One of the biggest challenges for entrepreneurs, especially those just starting out, is marketing with limited resources. You may not have the big budgets of established companies, but that doesn't mean you can't create effective marketing campaigns that drive growth. Hustlers know that it's not about how much money you spend—it's about how creative and strategic you are with what you have.

In this chapter, we'll explore low-cost, high-impact marketing strategies that will help you get the word out about your business without breaking the bank. From leveraging social media to grassroots outreach, you'll learn how to build awareness, attract customers, and grow your business on a shoestring budget.

1. Building a Strong Online Presence for Free

In today's digital world, having a strong online presence is crucial for any business. Fortunately, there are plenty of free tools and platforms that allow you to build your brand, reach new customers, and grow your audience without spending a dime.

How to Build a Strong Online Presence:

- **Leverage Social Media:** Platforms like Instagram, Facebook, Twitter, and LinkedIn are free to use and give you direct access to your target audience. Post regularly, engage with your followers, and use hashtags to increase your visibility. Sharing user-generated content or behind-the-scenes footage can make your brand more relatable and engaging.

- **Create a Website with Free Tools:** Websites are a must for establishing credibility. Use free website builders like **Wix** or **WordPress** to create a simple yet professional site. You can include a blog, product or service information, and ways for customers to contact or buy from you.

- **Start a Blog:** Blogging is a powerful way to attract visitors to your website, improve your SEO, and establish yourself as an expert in your industry. Write content that educates, informs, or entertains your audience. Not only will this build trust, but it will also help drive organic traffic to your site.

Free Marketing Hustle Tip:

Consistency is key. Even if you're using free tools, posting regularly and engaging with your audience will help you build momentum and increase your online presence over time.

2. Guerrilla Marketing: Creativity Over Budget

Guerrilla marketing is all about using creativity and unconventional tactics to promote your business. It's low-cost but high-impact, and the goal is to capture attention in unexpected ways. This approach works best when you want to stand out from the competition and make a lasting impression.

Guerrilla Marketing Ideas:

- **Street Art or Chalk Murals:** Create eye-catching, temporary street art or chalk murals in public spaces that feature your brand or message. Make sure to get any necessary permissions, but when done right, this can create buzz and encourage people to share on social media.
- **Flash Mobs or Pop-Up Events:** Organize a flash mob or pop-up event in a busy area to promote your product or service. These spontaneous and interactive experiences can attract attention and create a memorable brand impression.
- **Sticker Bombing:** Distribute branded stickers in high-traffic areas or place them in strategic locations. Stickers are cheap to produce but can go a long way in increasing brand awareness. Make sure to be mindful of where you place them to avoid legal issues.

Guerrilla Marketing Hustle Tip:

Think outside the box and tap into local communities. Guerrilla marketing works best when it's unexpected, memorable, and connected to the environment around you.

3. Word of Mouth: Turn Customers into Brand Advocates

Word-of-mouth marketing is one of the most powerful and cost-effective ways to grow your business. When customers recommend your products or services to their friends, family, or colleagues, it builds trust and credibility. The key to word-of-mouth success is delivering exceptional value and creating memorable experiences for your customers.

How to Encourage Word of Mouth:

- **Offer an Unforgettable Experience:** Go above and beyond in your customer service. Whether it's a handwritten thank-you note, surprise discounts, or personalized attention, small gestures can make a big impact and encourage people to talk about your brand.
- **Referral Programs:** Create a referral program that rewards customers for referring others to your business. You can offer discounts, free products, or even cash incentives. Platforms like **ReferralCandy** make it easy to set up referral programs online.
- **Ask for Reviews:** Encourage satisfied customers to leave reviews on platforms like Google, Yelp, or Trustpilot. Positive reviews not only build trust but also improve your online visibility and SEO.

Word of Mouth Hustle Tip:

Engage with your customers on social media, reply to comments, and share user-generated content. When people feel valued by your brand, they're more likely to recommend you to others.

4. Partnering with Local Businesses

Partnering with other local businesses is a great way to expand your reach without spending much money. By collaborating with complementary businesses, you can tap into their customer base while offering value to your own.

Ways to Partner with Local Businesses:

- **Co-Host Events:** Partner with another business to co-host an event, whether it's a workshop, networking mixer, or product launch. By sharing the costs and combining audiences, you can increase exposure for both brands.
- **Cross-Promotions:** Collaborate with businesses that serve a similar audience but offer different products or services. For example, if you run a coffee shop, partner with a local bakery to offer discounts when customers visit both locations.
- **Product or Service Bundles:** Create bundles or packages with other local businesses. For example, if you run a spa, you could partner with a local yoga studio to offer a "wellness day" package that includes both a yoga session and a massage.

Partnership Hustle Tip:

Focus on building win-win relationships. When both businesses benefit from the partnership, it's more likely to be successful and lead to long-term collaborations.

5. Email Marketing: High Impact, Low Cost

Email marketing is one of the most cost-effective ways to reach your audience directly. By building an email list of engaged customers, you can promote your products, share updates, and drive sales—all for minimal cost.

Steps to Build an Effective Email Marketing Strategy:

- **Build Your Email List:** Offer an incentive for people to sign up for your email list, such as a discount, free guide, or exclusive content. Make sure you collect emails from both your website visitors and customers.
- **Segment Your Audience:** Not all customers are the same, so don't treat them that way. Segment your email list based on customer behavior, preferences, or demographics. This allows you to send targeted messages that are more likely to convert.
- **Send Value-Driven Content:** Your emails shouldn't always be about selling. Mix in educational or entertaining content to keep your audience engaged. Provide tips, industry insights, or exclusive offers that add value to your subscribers.

Email Marketing Hustle Tip:

Automate your email campaigns using tools like **Mailchimp** or **ConvertKit**. This saves time and ensures that your subscribers are getting consistent communication from your brand.

6. Leveraging Community and Industry Groups

Engaging with local community groups, industry associations, or online forums is a powerful way to network and promote your business. By becoming an active participant in these groups, you can build relationships, gain exposure, and establish yourself as an expert in your field.

How to Leverage Community and Industry Groups:

- **Attend Local Meetups:** Whether it's industry-specific groups or general entrepreneur meetups, these events provide networking opportunities and allow you to share your expertise with others.
- **Offer Free Workshops or Webinars:** Hosting free workshops, webinars, or Q&A sessions within your community or industry can position you as an expert while providing valuable content to potential customers.
- **Engage in Online Communities:** Participate in online forums, Facebook groups, or Reddit communities related to your industry. Share advice, answer questions, and subtly promote your business when relevant.

Community Hustle Tip:

Offer value before promoting your business. Building trust and credibility in these groups will lead to organic opportunities for you to share your brand.

7. Creating Viral Content on a Budget

Viral content has the potential to skyrocket your brand's visibility overnight—and the best part is, it doesn't have to cost much. Whether it's a clever video, a meme, or a challenge, viral content captures people's attention and encourages them to share.

How to Create Viral Content:

- **Tap into Trends:** Keep an eye on current trends, challenges, and memes that are relevant to your audience. By creating content that aligns with popular trends, you increase your chances of going viral.
- **Use Humor or Emotion:** People are more likely to share content that makes them laugh or evokes strong emotions. Create content that resonates with your audience on a deeper level.
- **Encourage Participation:** Create challenges, contests, or prompts that encourage your audience to participate and share. For example, a social media challenge that ties into your brand can generate a wave of user-generated content.

Viral Content Hustle Tip:

Don't force it. The best viral content often comes from authenticity and tapping into something that naturally resonates with your audience.

8. Collaborating with Influencers

Influencer marketing doesn't always require a big budget. Many micro-influencers—those with smaller but highly engaged followings—are open to collaborating with small businesses. By partnering with influencers in your niche, you can reach a targeted audience and build credibility through word-of-mouth promotion.

How to Collaborate with Influencers on a Budget:

- **Find Micro-Influencers:** Micro-influencers (those with 1,000 to 100,000 followers) tend to have more engaged audiences and are often willing to

collaborate with small businesses in exchange for free products or services.

- **Offer Free Products or Services:** Instead of paying influencers in cash, offer them free products, services, or exclusive experiences in exchange for a shout-out or review. Many influencers appreciate the opportunity to showcase unique, high-quality brands to their audience.
- **Create Long-Term Partnerships:** Rather than one-off collaborations, focus on building long-term relationships with influencers who genuinely love your brand. These partnerships often lead to more authentic and effective promotion over time.

Influencer Hustle Tip:

Research influencers carefully. Look for people whose values align with your brand and who have an audience that fits your target market.

Marketing on a budget doesn't mean sacrificing results. By getting creative, leveraging free tools, and focusing on authentic relationships, you can spread the word about your business without spending a fortune. The key is to be strategic, stay consistent, and always look for ways to add value to your audience.

Next Chapter: Now that you've mastered budget-friendly marketing strategies, it's time to learn how to handle setbacks and failures. In the next chapter, we'll explore how to turn losses into lessons and bounce back stronger than ever.

14

Chapter 14

Chapter 14: Dealing with Setbacks and Failures

Turning Losses into Lessons and Bouncing Back Stronger

Every entrepreneur, no matter how talented or experienced, will face setbacks and failures. It's part of the journey. But what separates successful entrepreneurs from the rest is how they respond to challenges. Setbacks are inevitable, but they can be powerful learning opportunities that propel you forward—if you handle them right.

In this chapter, we'll explore how to deal with failures and bounce back even stronger. You'll learn how to turn losses into valuable lessons, build resilience, and develop the mental toughness needed to keep pushing forward when things go wrong. The hustle isn't about avoiding failure—it's about learning how to use it to fuel your growth.

1. Embracing Failure as Part of the Process

Failure is an unavoidable part of the entrepreneurial journey, and the key to overcoming it lies in your mindset. You must learn to see failure not as a defeat, but as a stepping stone to success. Every successful entrepreneur has experienced failure at some point, and those failures shaped their eventual victories.

Why Failure is a Valuable Teacher:

- **It Builds Resilience:** Facing setbacks teaches you how to adapt, persevere, and keep moving forward, even when the road gets tough. It builds the mental and emotional strength you need to handle future challenges.
- **It Provides Clarity:** Failure often forces you to take a closer look at what's not working in your business. It provides clarity on weak points, ineffective strategies, or poor decisions, allowing you to make more informed choices moving forward.
- **It Drives Innovation:** Many great ideas and innovations are born out of failure. When something doesn't work, it pushes you to think creatively, test new ideas, and come up with better solutions.

Failure Hustle Tip:

Don't let the fear of failure hold you back. The biggest failure is not trying at all. Every mistake you make brings you closer to finding what works.

2. Analyzing the Failure: What Went Wrong?

When a setback happens, it's important to take a step back and analyze what went wrong. Without understanding the root cause, you risk making the same mistake again. Instead of dwelling on the failure, use it as an opportunity for introspection and improvement.

How to Analyze a Failure:

- **Ask the Right Questions:** Break down the situation by asking key questions like: What was the original goal? What steps did you take? Where did things start to go off track? Were there external factors that contributed? These questions help you identify the underlying issues.
- **Seek Feedback:** Sometimes, an outside perspective can reveal blind spots you might have missed. Talk to your team, mentors, or customers to gather feedback. They might offer insights that help you see the failure from a new angle.
- **Identify Patterns:** If you've faced multiple setbacks, look for recurring patterns. Are there consistent issues with your strategy, execution, or decision-making? Recognizing patterns allows you to adjust your approach and avoid similar mistakes in the future.

Analysis Hustle Tip:

Failure isn't the end of the road; it's the start of a new chapter. The sooner you understand what went wrong, the sooner you can fix it and move forward stronger.

3. Developing Resilience: The Key to Bouncing Back

Resilience is one of the most important traits any entrepreneur can develop. It's the ability to recover from setbacks, adapt to challenges, and keep pushing forward. Developing resilience doesn't mean ignoring failures; it means facing them head-on and using them as motivation to grow.

How to Build Resilience:

- **Reframe Setbacks as Learning Opportunities:** Instead of seeing failures as defeats, reframe them as valuable lessons. Each setback provides insights that can help you improve your business and sharpen your skills.
- **Focus on What You Can Control:** While some factors are beyond your control, there's always something you can change or improve. Focus on what you can control—your mindset, your actions, and your response to challenges.
- **Practice Self-Care:** Resilience isn't just about mental toughness—it's also about taking care of your physical and emotional well-being. Make sure you're getting enough rest, managing stress, and maintaining a healthy work-life balance. The stronger you are, the better you'll be able to handle setbacks.

Resilience Hustle Tip:

Resilience is like a muscle—the more you work it, the stronger it gets. Each time you bounce back from a setback, you're building the strength to handle future challenges with confidence.

4. Learning from Setbacks: Turning Losses into Lessons

The most successful entrepreneurs don't just move on from failures—they actively learn from them. Each setback contains valuable lessons that, when applied, can help you avoid future mistakes and become a better entrepreneur.

Steps to Turn Setbacks into Lessons:

- **Identify the Key Takeaways:** Once you've analyzed the failure, focus on the specific lessons you've learned. Did you misjudge the market? Did you overlook a key customer need? Write down the lessons and use them to adjust your approach.
- **Apply the Lessons to Your Next Move:** Use what you've learned to inform your next steps. Whether it's refining your strategy, improving your product, or adjusting your marketing approach, make sure you're applying those lessons to avoid repeating mistakes.
- **Share the Lessons with Your Team:** If you have a team, share the lessons you've learned. This not only helps improve the entire team's approach moving forward but also fosters a culture of growth and learning within your business.

Learning Hustle Tip:

Failures are only wasted if you don't learn from them. Treat every setback as a valuable lesson that brings you closer to success.

5. Pivoting After a Failure

Sometimes a setback is a sign that you need to pivot. Pivoting doesn't mean giving up on your original idea—it means adapting your strategy based on new insights or circumstances. Whether it's changing your product, your target market, or your entire business model, pivoting can be the key to unlocking new opportunities.

How to Pivot After a Setback:

- **Reassess Your Business Model:** If your current business model isn't working, take a step back and reassess. Look for new opportunities in your market or consider different revenue models that might better align with customer needs.
- **Adjust Your Target Audience:** If your product or service isn't resonating with your current audience, consider targeting a different demographic. Sometimes, a small shift in focus can lead to a big breakthrough.

- **Test and Iterate:** Before fully committing to a new direction, test your ideas on a small scale. Whether it's a new marketing campaign or a revised product, gather feedback and iterate based on the results.

Pivoting Hustle Tip:

Don't be afraid to let go of what's not working. The sooner you pivot, the sooner you can focus on what will move your business forward.

6. Rebuilding Confidence After a Failure

Failure can take a toll on your confidence, but it's important to rebuild and keep moving forward. Confidence is essential for taking risks, making bold decisions, and inspiring your team or customers. After a setback, it's crucial to remind yourself of your strengths and successes.

How to Rebuild Confidence:

- **Celebrate Small Wins:** Focus on the small victories. Each step forward, no matter how minor, is progress. Celebrate these moments to remind yourself that you're still on the right track.
- **Reflect on Past Successes:** Take time to reflect on your past achievements. Remember the times you've overcome challenges, and use those experiences to rebuild your confidence. You've succeeded before, and you will again.
- **Surround Yourself with Support:** Lean on your mentors, team, or fellow entrepreneurs for encouragement and support. Sometimes, having people in your corner who believe in you can help rebuild your belief in yourself.

Confidence Hustle Tip:

Confidence isn't about never failing—it's about knowing you have the strength to keep going, no matter what setbacks come your way.

7. Moving Forward: Building on Failure for Future Success

Once you've analyzed the failure, applied the lessons, and rebuilt your confidence, it's time to move forward. Don't let fear of future setbacks hold you back. Instead, use your past failures as a foundation for future success.

How to Move Forward After Failure:

- **Set New Goals:** Use what you've learned from the setback to set new, more informed goals. These goals should be realistic but ambitious enough to push you out of your comfort zone.
- **Take Calculated Risks:** Don't shy away from taking risks just because you've experienced failure. The most successful entrepreneurs take calculated risks based on their knowledge, experience, and the lessons they've learned.
- **Keep Learning and Adapting:** The hustle never stops, and neither should your learning. Stay curious, continue refining your strategies, and be open to new opportunities and challenges.

Moving Forward Hustle Tip:

Failure isn't the opposite of success—it's part of the process. Every setback brings you one step closer to where you want to be, as long as you keep moving forward.

Setbacks and failures are inevitable, but they don't have to define your journey. By embracing failure as part of the process, learning from your mistakes, and building resilience, you can turn every loss into a stepping stone toward greater success. The hustle is about perseverance, and each failure is just another step toward your ultimate goals.

Next Chapter: Now that you've learned how to deal with setbacks, it's time to focus on scaling your hustle. In the next chapter, we'll explore how to transition from a side hustle to a full-fledged enterprise and take your business to the next level.

Chapter 15

Chapter 15: Scaling Your Hustle

Transitioning from a Side Hustle to a Full-Fledged Enterprise

Turning a side hustle into a full-fledged enterprise is a major milestone in any entrepreneur's journey. It's the point where your business evolves from something you do in your spare time into a thriving operation that demands full focus and provides sustainable income. Scaling your hustle is about more than just working harder—it's about working smarter, building systems, and laying the foundation for long-term growth.

In this chapter, we'll explore the steps to transition your side hustle into a full-fledged business. You'll learn how to grow your operations, expand your customer base, and build the infrastructure needed to support a scalable, sustainable enterprise. Scaling isn't just about growing—it's about growing strategically.

1. Knowing When It's Time to Scale

Scaling your business requires both readiness and timing. If you grow too fast without the right systems in place, you risk burning out or collapsing under the pressure. On the other hand, waiting too long to scale can lead to missed opportunities and stagnation.

Signs You're Ready to Scale:

- **Consistent Revenue:** If your side hustle is generating consistent income and you have a clear path to profitability, it may be time to scale. Steady cash flow is a key indicator that your business is ready for growth.

- **Demand Exceeds Capacity:** If you're struggling to keep up with demand, it's a sign that your business is ready to expand. When customers are lining up faster than you can serve them, it's time to grow your operations.

- **You've Outgrown Part-Time Status:** If your side hustle is taking up most of your time and attention, and you're consistently juggling it with your main job, scaling may be the next step toward making it your full-time focus.

Scaling Hustle Tip:

Scaling should be driven by demand, not ambition. Ensure there's a clear need in the market for your product or service before investing in growth.

2. Building Scalable Systems and Processes

One of the key differences between a side hustle and a full-fledged business is the systems and processes that support it. A scalable business has efficient, repeatable systems that allow it to grow without requiring you to handle every aspect personally.

How to Build Scalable Systems:

- **Document Your Processes:** Write down every step involved in running your business, from customer acquisition to product delivery. This documentation will be invaluable when you begin delegating tasks to others.
- **Automate Where Possible:** Use tools and software to automate repetitive tasks like invoicing, customer follow-ups, and social media scheduling. Automation saves time and ensures consistency as you scale.
- **Outsource or Delegate:** As your business grows, you won't be able to handle everything yourself. Identify tasks that can be outsourced or delegated to team members or freelancers. Focus your energy on high-impact areas like strategy, leadership, and business development.

Systems Hustle Tip:

Don't wait until you're overwhelmed to start building systems. Put processes in place early so you can scale smoothly as demand increases.

3. Expanding Your Customer Base

To scale your business, you'll need to grow your customer base. Expanding beyond your current market is essential for long-term growth and sustainability. Whether through new marketing strategies, product diversification, or entering new geographical areas, scaling requires you to reach a larger audience.

Strategies for Expanding Your Customer Base:

- **Refine Your Marketing:** Invest in more targeted marketing efforts to reach new customers. Use tools like Google Ads, Facebook Ads, or SEO to attract a larger audience. As you grow, consider hiring a marketing specialist or agency to help you refine and execute your strategy.
- **Leverage Customer Referrals:** Word of mouth is one of the most powerful marketing tools. Encourage your existing customers to refer friends or colleagues through a referral program that rewards them for bringing in new business.

- **Enter New Markets:** If your business is currently serving a local or niche audience, consider expanding to new geographic locations or customer segments. This could involve launching an e-commerce site, attending trade shows, or entering international markets.

Customer Growth Hustle Tip:

Focus on retaining your current customers as you scale. Customer loyalty and repeat business are just as important as acquiring new customers, especially when expanding.

4. Securing Funding for Growth

Scaling often requires investment—whether it's to hire new staff, invest in equipment, or expand your marketing efforts. If your business is profitable, you may be able to reinvest your earnings, but if you need additional funding, there are several options available.

Ways to Secure Funding for Scaling:

- **Reinvest Profits:** If your side hustle is generating a profit, consider reinvesting those earnings back into the business. This allows you to grow without taking on debt or giving up equity.
- **Small Business Loans:** Many financial institutions offer small business loans for entrepreneurs looking to scale. These loans can provide the capital needed for hiring, expanding operations, or purchasing equipment.
- **Crowdfunding:** If your product has a strong appeal to consumers, consider using platforms like **Kickstarter** or **Indiegogo** to raise funds. Crowdfunding can help you raise capital while also building a loyal customer base.
- **Angel Investors or Venture Capital:** For businesses with high growth potential, seeking investment from angel investors or venture capital firms might be an option. This often involves giving up some equity in exchange for significant funding.

Funding Hustle Tip:

Be strategic about your funding sources. Only take on debt or give up equity if it's absolutely necessary and aligns with your long-term goals.

5. Building a Team to Support Your Growth

As your business grows, so will your need for help. Scaling requires you to go from being a solopreneur to building and managing a team. Hiring the right people is critical to maintaining quality, meeting customer demand, and growing your operations.

How to Build a Team for Scaling:

- **Hire for Key Roles First:** Identify the most important roles you need to fill, such as operations, customer service, or marketing. Start with these key hires to help manage the essential aspects of your business.

- **Look for Cultural Fit:** As important as skills are, cultural fit is just as critical. You want to build a team that shares your vision and values. This ensures everyone is working toward the same goals and fosters a positive work environment.
- **Invest in Training:** When hiring new team members, take the time to train them properly. Make sure they understand your processes, customer expectations, and company culture. A well-trained team is key to maintaining quality and efficiency as you scale.

Team-Building Hustle Tip:

Don't rush the hiring process. Take your time to find the right people who will contribute to your long-term growth and success.

6. Maintaining Quality and Consistency

One of the biggest challenges when scaling a business is maintaining the quality and consistency that made your side hustle successful in the first place. As you grow, it's easy for quality to slip, especially when you're no longer handling everything personally.

How to Maintain Quality While Scaling:

- **Standardize Your Processes:** Document and standardize every process that affects the customer experience, from production to customer service. This ensures consistency even as you grow.
- **Set Clear Expectations:** Whether it's for your team, suppliers, or partners, make sure everyone understands the standards you've set for quality. Regularly communicate your expectations and hold people accountable for meeting them.
- **Monitor Customer Feedback:** Keep a close eye on customer feedback as you scale. If you notice recurring issues or complaints, address them immediately. Customer satisfaction should remain a top priority, no matter how fast you're growing.

Quality Hustle Tip:

Make quality part of your company culture. If everyone on your team is committed to maintaining high standards, it will be easier to uphold quality as you scale.

7. Scaling Sustainably

Growing too fast can lead to burnout, financial strain, or operational breakdowns. Scaling your business sustainably means growing at a pace that allows you to maintain control, protect your resources, and ensure long-term success.

How to Scale Sustainably:

- **Pace Your Growth:** Don't try to scale everything at once. Focus on one area of growth at a time, whether it's expanding your product line, entering new markets, or building your team. This controlled approach will prevent overwhelm and allow you to manage growth effectively.

- **Monitor Your Cash Flow:** As you scale, it's easy for expenses to outpace revenue. Keep a close eye on your cash flow to ensure that you have enough working capital to support your growth without running into financial trouble.
- **Stay True to Your Core Values:** Don't lose sight of the values and mission that made your side hustle successful. As you grow, make sure your brand remains authentic and connected to your original vision.

Sustainability Hustle Tip:

Growing a business is a marathon, not a sprint. Focus on building a strong foundation for long-term success rather than chasing rapid, unsustainable growth.

8. Transitioning to Full-Time Entrepreneurship

Scaling your side hustle often means making the leap to full-time entrepreneurship. This is a big step, and while it can be exciting, it also comes with its own set of challenges. The key is to plan your transition carefully to ensure a smooth shift from part-time hustle to full-time enterprise.

Steps to Transition to Full-Time:

- **Build a Financial Cushion:** Before quitting your day job, make sure you have a financial safety net. Aim for at least six months of living expenses saved up to cover any unexpected challenges during the transition.
- **Time Your Exit:** Don't rush into leaving your job. Wait until your side hustle is consistently generating enough revenue to support your lifestyle. If you're confident in your business's stability

, you'll feel more secure making the leap.

- **Prepare for a Shift in Mindset:** Full-time entrepreneurship requires a shift in mindset. You'll no longer have the security of a steady paycheck, but you'll gain the freedom to fully invest in your business. Be prepared for the emotional and mental challenges that come with this new chapter.

Full-Time Hustle Tip:

Trust in your ability to make your business work, but be strategic in your approach. A well-planned transition will set you up for long-term success as a full-time entrepreneur.

Scaling your hustle is an exciting but challenging process. It requires strategic planning, efficient systems, and a commitment to maintaining quality as you grow. By expanding your customer base, building a strong team, and managing your growth sustainably, you can turn your side hustle into a thriving full-fledged business.

Next Chapter: Now that you've learned how to scale your hustle, it's time to explore the legal aspects of running a full-fledged business. In the next chapter, we'll cover business registration, contracts, and compliance to ensure your business is operating legally and securely.

Chapter 16

Chapter 16: Navigating the Legal Landscape

Registering Your Business, Contracts, and Compliance

Scaling your hustle into a full-fledged business is an exciting milestone, but with growth comes the need to address the legal aspects of running a company. Properly structuring your business, ensuring legal compliance, and protecting your interests are crucial steps in building a sustainable enterprise. Navigating the legal landscape can feel overwhelming, but taking the time to get it right will save you from future headaches.

In this chapter, we'll dive into the essential legal considerations for any entrepreneur. From choosing the right business structure to understanding contracts and staying compliant with regulations, you'll learn how to protect your business and ensure that it's legally sound as you scale.

1. Choosing the Right Business Structure

One of the first legal decisions you'll need to make when transitioning from a side hustle to a full business is selecting the right business structure. The structure you choose will affect everything from your taxes to your personal liability.

Common Business Structures:

- **Sole Proprietorship:** The simplest form of business, a sole proprietorship means you're the sole owner. However, you're personally liable for all the business's debts and obligations. While this is often fine for side hustles, it's risky for a growing business.
- **Limited Liability Company (LLC):** An LLC provides liability protection, meaning your personal assets are separate from the business. This is a popular option for small business owners because it offers flexibility in management and tax treatment.
- **S Corporation (S Corp):** An S Corp provides liability protection like an LLC but comes with certain tax benefits, such as avoiding self-employment taxes on profits. However, there are more regulations, and you must pay yourself a reasonable salary.

- **C Corporation (C Corp):** A C Corp is a separate legal entity from its owners, offering liability protection and easier access to investors. However, it comes with double taxation (profits are taxed at the corporate level and again when distributed to shareholders).

Business Structure Hustle Tip:

Consult with a legal or financial professional to help you determine which structure best suits your business goals and growth plans.

2. Registering Your Business

Once you've chosen a business structure, the next step is registering your business. This ensures that your business is recognized as a legal entity and is compliant with local, state, and federal regulations.

Steps to Register Your Business:

1. **Choose a Business Name:** Your business name should be unique and not already in use by another company in your state. Conduct a name search through your state's business registry to ensure it's available.
2. **Register Your Business with the State:** Depending on your chosen business structure, you'll need to register with your state's Secretary of State office. For LLCs and corporations, this often involves filing Articles of Organization or Incorporation.
3. **Get an Employer Identification Number (EIN):** An EIN is a tax ID number for your business. You can apply for one online through the IRS website. This is required if you have employees or operate as a corporation or partnership.
4. **Obtain Any Necessary Licenses or Permits:** Depending on your industry and location, you may need specific licenses or permits to operate legally. This could include business licenses, health permits, or zoning approvals.

Registration Hustle Tip:

Registering your business not only makes it official but also builds credibility with customers, investors, and partners. Make sure your business name, domain name, and social media handles are aligned for brand consistency.

3. Understanding Contracts and Agreements

As your business grows, you'll likely enter into contracts with clients, vendors, employees, and partners. Contracts are essential to protecting your interests and ensuring that everyone involved understands their responsibilities.

Key Types of Contracts:

- **Client Contracts:** Outline the terms of your work, including deliverables, payment terms, timelines, and intellectual property rights. Clear contracts help avoid misunderstandings and ensure both parties are aligned.

- **Employee and Contractor Agreements:** Whether hiring employees or working with independent contractors, it's crucial to have clear contracts that outline expectations, compensation, and confidentiality. This protects both your business and the people you hire.
- **Non-Disclosure Agreements (NDAs):** An NDA ensures that sensitive information shared during business dealings remains confidential. This is especially important when discussing proprietary information with potential partners, employees, or investors.
- **Partnership Agreements:** If you're partnering with another individual or business, a partnership agreement outlines each party's roles, responsibilities, profit sharing, and what happens if the partnership dissolves.

Contracts Hustle Tip:

Never rely on verbal agreements. Always get agreements in writing to protect yourself legally. If necessary, consult a lawyer to ensure your contracts are comprehensive and enforceable.

4. Protecting Your Intellectual Property

Your business's intellectual property (IP) includes things like your brand name, logo, product designs, and proprietary technology. Protecting your IP ensures that no one can use or copy your ideas without permission, safeguarding the value you've built in your business.

Types of Intellectual Property Protection:

- **Trademarks:** A trademark protects your brand's name, logo, and slogan. Registering a trademark with the U.S. Patent and Trademark Office (USPTO) gives you exclusive rights to use those elements in your industry.
- **Copyrights:** Copyright protection applies to original works of authorship, such as written content, music, and software. It automatically applies upon creation, but registering a copyright provides additional legal protection.
- **Patents:** If you've developed a new product, invention, or process, a patent gives you the exclusive right to make, use, or sell that invention for a specified period.
- **Trade Secrets:** If your business relies on confidential formulas, processes, or customer lists, you can protect these as trade secrets. This involves keeping the information confidential and using NDAs with employees or partners who have access to the information.

Intellectual Property Hustle Tip:

If your business relies heavily on branding, original content, or innovation, protecting your IP should be a priority. Consider consulting with an IP lawyer to develop a strategy that works for your business.

5. Staying Compliant with Regulations

As your business grows, it's important to stay compliant with local, state, and federal regulations. Failing to comply with business laws can result in fines, legal disputes, or even the shutdown of your business. Understanding and following these regulations will ensure your business operates smoothly and legally.

Common Areas of Compliance:

- **Taxes:** Ensure you're filing the appropriate business taxes, including income tax, sales tax, payroll tax, and any other taxes that apply to your business. Hire a qualified accountant to help manage your finances and file taxes correctly.
- **Employment Laws:** If you're hiring employees, familiarize yourself with labor laws, including minimum wage, overtime pay, employee benefits, and workplace safety regulations.
- **Health and Safety Regulations:** Depending on your industry, there may be specific health and safety regulations you need to follow. For example, restaurants must meet health department standards, while manufacturing companies must follow OSHA guidelines.
- **Data Privacy Laws:** If your business collects customer data, you must comply with data privacy laws such as the General Data Protection Regulation (GDPR) in the EU or the California Consumer Privacy Act (CCPA) in the U.S. Make sure you have clear data privacy policies in place and take steps to protect customer information.

Compliance Hustle Tip:

Stay informed about changes in regulations that affect your industry. Consider working with legal and financial professionals to ensure your business stays compliant as it grows.

6. Protecting Yourself and Your Business

As your business expands, so do the risks. Protecting yourself and your business from liability is essential to long-term success. This includes having the right insurance coverage and building a business structure that separates your personal assets from business liabilities.

Ways to Protect Your Business:

- **Business Insurance:** Depending on your industry, you may need general liability insurance, professional liability insurance, or product liability insurance. These policies protect you from lawsuits, accidents, or damages that could otherwise cripple your business.
- **Workers' Compensation Insurance:** If you have employees, workers' compensation insurance is often required by law. It covers medical expenses and lost wages for employees who are injured on the job.
- **Personal Liability Protection:** If you've registered your business as an LLC or corporation, your personal assets are protected from business debts and lawsuits. This shields your personal savings, home, and other assets from being at risk if your business faces legal issues.

Protection Hustle Tip:

Review your insurance needs regularly as your business grows and evolves. What worked for your small side hustle may not be enough to protect your business as it scales.

7. Preparing for Future Growth: Legal Considerations

As you scale your business, it's important to consider future legal needs. Whether you're planning to bring on investors, expand internationally, or sell your company, legal preparation is key to smooth growth and exit strategies.

Legal Considerations for Future Growth:

- **Equity Agreements:** If you plan to bring on investors, partners, or co-founders, clear equity agreements are crucial. These agreements outline ownership stakes, voting rights, and what happens in the event of an exit or dissolution.
- **Expansion Plans:** If you plan to expand internationally or into new markets, understand the legal regulations of those regions. This could include trade laws, foreign investment regulations, or licensing requirements.
- **Exit Strategy:** Even if you're not planning to sell your business right now, it's important to have a clear exit strategy. Whether you plan to pass the business on to family, sell to an investor, or merge with another company, having legal structures in place will make the process smoother.

Growth Hustle Tip:

Future-proof your business by preparing for growth early. Stay proactive about legal matters to ensure you're ready for whatever opportunities or challenges come your way.

Navigating the legal landscape is essential to scaling your hustle into a legitimate, thriving enterprise. By choosing the right business structure, protecting your intellectual property, and staying compliant with regulations, you'll build a solid foundation for long-term success. Legal preparation isn't just about avoiding problems—it's about positioning your business for sustainable growth.

Next Chapter: Now that you've secured the legal foundation for your business, it's time to dive into developing a robust customer acquisition strategy. In the next chapter, we'll explore ways to attract, engage, and retain customers as you scale your enterprise.

Chapter 17

Chapter 17: Crafting a Customer Acquisition Strategy

Attracting, Engaging, and Retaining Customers as You Scale

A business is only as strong as its customers. No matter how great your product or service is, without customers, your business can't survive. As you scale your hustle, developing a robust customer acquisition strategy is crucial to maintaining growth and building long-term success. Attracting new customers, engaging them effectively, and retaining them for the long haul requires a well-thought-out plan that balances marketing, customer experience, and relationship building.

In this chapter, we'll explore how to create a customer acquisition strategy that not only brings new clients to your business but also turns them into loyal customers who drive ongoing growth. From building awareness and nurturing leads to creating lasting relationships, this chapter will guide you through every step of the customer journey.

1. Defining Your Ideal Customer

Before you can attract customers, you need to know who you're targeting. Defining your ideal customer (also known as your customer persona) is the first step in crafting a customer acquisition strategy that works. Understanding your audience's needs, pain points, and behaviors will allow you to tailor your marketing efforts and deliver value that resonates.

How to Define Your Ideal Customer:

- **Demographics:** Consider your ideal customer's age, gender, income level, location, and occupation. These details help narrow down your target audience and focus your marketing on the right people.
- **Psychographics:** Go beyond demographics by analyzing your customers' behaviors, values, and motivations. What are their goals? What problems are they trying to solve? How does your product or service fit into their lives?
- **Customer Pain Points:** Identify the key challenges your ideal customers face. Whether it's convenience, cost, or inefficiency, understanding these pain points will help you position your product or service as the solution.

- **Buyer Journey:** Understand the different stages your ideal customer goes through before making a purchase. Are they conducting research, comparing options, or ready to buy? Tailor your messaging to where they are in the buying process.

Customer Persona Hustle Tip:

Create multiple customer personas to represent different segments of your audience. This allows you to customize your marketing strategy for each group and increase the effectiveness of your campaigns.

2. Building Brand Awareness: Getting Your Name Out There

The first step in customer acquisition is making sure people know your business exists. Brand awareness is about increasing your visibility and ensuring your brand is recognizable to your target audience. Whether through social media, content marketing, or partnerships, building awareness is the foundation of any acquisition strategy.

Ways to Build Brand Awareness:

- **Content Marketing:** Create valuable content that educates, informs, or entertains your audience. Blog posts, videos, infographics, and podcasts are all effective ways to showcase your expertise and attract attention.
- **Social Media:** Use platforms like Instagram, LinkedIn, Facebook, and Twitter to engage with your audience and build relationships. Post regularly, share user-generated content, and participate in industry conversations to increase your reach.
- **Paid Advertising:** If you have a budget, paid advertising on platforms like Google Ads, Facebook Ads, or Instagram Ads can quickly boost your visibility. Target your ads to reach your ideal customers and drive traffic to your website or landing pages.
- **Collaborations and Partnerships:** Partner with other businesses, influencers, or industry leaders to increase your brand's visibility. Cross-promotions, guest blogging, and co-hosting events are powerful ways to introduce your brand to a new audience.

Brand Awareness Hustle Tip:

Stay consistent with your messaging and visuals across all platforms. A cohesive brand presence makes your business more memorable and recognizable to potential customers.

3. Generating Leads: Turning Awareness into Interest

Once you've built brand awareness, the next step is to turn that awareness into interest. Lead generation involves capturing the attention of potential customers and guiding them toward taking action, whether that's signing up for a newsletter, requesting a consultation, or following your social media accounts.

Lead Generation Strategies:

- **Lead Magnets:** Offer something of value in exchange for a potential customer's contact information. This could be a free ebook, discount code, webinar, or other resource that appeals to your target audience.
- **Landing Pages:** Create dedicated landing pages designed to capture leads. These pages should be clear, focused, and include a strong call to action, such as "Sign Up Now" or "Get Your Free Guide."
- **Email Opt-ins:** Encourage website visitors to subscribe to your email list by offering exclusive content, promotions, or updates. Building an email list gives you a direct line of communication with potential customers.
- **Retargeting Ads:** Use retargeting ads to engage visitors who have previously interacted with your website or social media. These ads remind potential customers about your brand and encourage them to return and complete their purchase.

Lead Generation Hustle Tip:

Use A/B testing to experiment with different headlines, offers, and designs for your lead generation campaigns. Testing helps you identify what resonates most with your audience and optimize for better results.

4. Nurturing Leads: Building Relationships with Potential Customers

Not every lead will convert into a paying customer right away. Nurturing leads is about building relationships over time and guiding them through the buying process. This involves educating your prospects, addressing their concerns, and keeping your brand top of mind until they're ready to make a purchase.

Lead Nurturing Tactics:

- **Email Campaigns:** Send personalized email campaigns that deliver value to your leads. Share educational content, success stories, and testimonials that demonstrate how your product or service solves their problems.
- **Social Proof:** Use customer reviews, testimonials, and case studies to build trust with your leads. Seeing that others have had positive experiences with your brand can reassure potential customers and move them closer to a purchase.
- **Content Drip Campaigns:** Develop a series of automated emails that gradually introduce your leads to your product or service. Each email should provide valuable insights or information, building trust and interest over time.
- **Live Chat and Support:** Offering real-time support through live chat can help address any concerns or questions your leads may have. This direct interaction can be the difference between a lost lead and a converted customer.

Lead Nurturing Hustle Tip:

Focus on providing value at every touchpoint. Instead of pushing for a sale, offer solutions, insights, and advice that genuinely help your leads. This builds trust and positions you as the go-to solution when they're ready to buy.

5. Converting Leads into Paying Customers

After nurturing your leads, the next step is conversion. Turning interested prospects into paying customers requires a compelling offer, clear value propositions, and a seamless buying experience. The easier and more appealing you make it for customers to purchase, the higher your conversion rates will be.

Strategies for Converting Leads:

- **Create a Strong Call to Action (CTA):** Make it clear what you want your leads to do next, whether it's booking a consultation, signing up for a trial, or making a purchase. Your CTA should be bold, direct, and aligned with the lead's needs.
- **Offer Time-Sensitive Deals:** Creating a sense of urgency through limited-time offers or discounts can encourage leads to take action. Whether it's a holiday sale, early-bird special, or flash sale, time-sensitive offers create excitement and drive conversions.
- **Simplify the Buying Process:** Ensure that your website or sales funnel is easy to navigate. Reduce friction in the buying process by simplifying checkout, offering multiple payment options, and minimizing unnecessary steps.
- **Follow Up with Abandoned Carts:** If you have an e-commerce business, use email reminders to follow up with customers who added items to their cart but didn't complete the purchase. Offering a small discount or free shipping can incentivize them to return and finish the transaction.

Conversion Hustle Tip:

Track your conversion metrics and optimize based on performance. Whether it's your email open rates, click-through rates, or sales conversion rates, understanding where prospects drop off will help you improve your process.

6. Retaining Customers: Building Loyalty for Long-Term Growth

Customer acquisition is just the beginning. Retaining customers and building loyalty is where true growth happens. Loyal customers not only provide repeat business but also become brand advocates who refer new clients to your business. The key is to create an exceptional experience that keeps customers coming back.

Customer Retention Strategies:

- **Deliver Exceptional Customer Service:** Providing outstanding customer service sets you apart from the competition and ensures your customers feel valued. Respond promptly to inquiries, address concerns, and go the extra mile to exceed expectations.

- **Loyalty Programs:** Reward your customers for their loyalty with special discounts, exclusive offers, or a points-based system that gives them perks for repeat purchases.
- **Stay Engaged:** Continue to nurture relationships with your existing customers through regular email updates, personalized offers, or VIP access to new products. Keeping in touch ensures they feel connected to your brand even after the initial purchase.
- **Collect and Act on Feedback:** Regularly ask for feedback from your customers and use it to improve your products, services, and customer experience. Showing that you listen and act on feedback strengthens trust and loyalty.

Customer Retention Hustle Tip:

The cost of acquiring a new customer is higher than retaining an existing one. Focus on keeping your customers happy, and they'll continue to support your business for years to come.

7. Measuring and Optimizing Your Customer Acquisition Strategy

A successful customer acquisition strategy isn't static—it evolves over time based on data, performance, and customer feedback. Regularly measuring your results and optimizing your approach ensures that you're maximizing your acquisition efforts and continually improving.

Key Metrics to Track:

- **Customer Acquisition Cost (CAC):** How much are you spending to acquire each customer? Keeping your CAC low is essential for maintaining profitability.
- **Customer Lifetime Value (CLTV):** How much revenue does each customer generate over their lifetime with your business? A high CLTV means that your customers are valuable and loyal.
- **Conversion Rate:** What percentage of your leads are converting into paying customers? Optimizing your conversion rate will help you get the most out of your acquisition efforts.
- **Retention Rate:** How many of your customers stick around and make repeat purchases? A strong retention rate indicates that your customer experience is effective.

Optimization Hustle Tip:

Use data to identify weak points in your acquisition funnel. Whether it's lead generation, nurturing, or conversion, continuous optimization will help you fine-tune your strategy and maximize results.

Crafting an effective customer acquisition strategy is essential to scaling your hustle. By defining your ideal customer, building awareness, nurturing leads, and focusing on retention, you'll create a pipeline of loyal customers who fuel your business's growth. Remember, it's not just about acquiring customers—it's about turning them into lifelong supporters of your brand.

Next Chapter: Now that you've mastered customer acquisition, it's time to explore the art of scaling your operations. In the next chapter, we'll dive into how to optimize your internal processes and grow your team for sustainable expansion.

18

Chapter 18

Chapter 18: Scaling Your Operations

Optimizing Internal Processes and Growing Your Team for Sustainable Expansion

As your business grows, so do the complexities of managing day-to-day operations. Scaling your operations effectively is essential to maintaining the quality, efficiency, and productivity that your business was built on. It's not enough to simply hire more people or expand your production capacity—successful scaling requires optimizing internal processes, establishing a scalable infrastructure, and fostering a strong company culture.

In this chapter, we'll dive into how to streamline operations, build a robust infrastructure, and expand your team to support long-term growth. You'll learn how to maintain control while scaling, ensuring your business can handle increasing demands without losing sight of its core values and customer promise.

1. Streamlining Processes: The Foundation of Scaling

At the heart of any scalable business is efficiency. As your company grows, your processes must be streamlined to handle more customers, more products, and more services—without increasing overhead costs disproportionately. Streamlining your operations ensures that you can meet demand, reduce bottlenecks, and improve overall productivity.

How to Streamline Your Operations:

- **Document Every Process:** Start by documenting all key processes within your business—from sales and marketing to product development and customer service. This documentation creates a blueprint that you can refine, optimize, and pass on as you scale.

- **Automate Repetitive Tasks:** Use automation tools to handle repetitive tasks like data entry, invoicing, social media scheduling, and email marketing. Automation frees up time for you and your team to focus on higher-level, strategic tasks.

- **Eliminate Redundancies:** Analyze your current workflows to identify unnecessary steps or redundant processes. Simplify and consolidate wherever possible to create a more efficient operation.

- **Invest in Software Solutions:** The right software tools can dramatically improve efficiency. Whether it's a customer relationship management (CRM) system, project management tool, or accounting software, investing in technology helps keep your business organized and scalable.

Process Optimization Hustle Tip:

Start with the processes that are most critical to your business. If you're in e-commerce, focus on streamlining order fulfillment and customer service. If you offer services, streamline scheduling, communication, and billing.

2. Building Scalable Infrastructure

As you grow, your business will require a more robust infrastructure to support increased demand. This includes everything from your digital systems and software to your physical space and equipment. A scalable infrastructure ensures that your business can handle growth without breaking down or creating inefficiencies.

Key Areas of Infrastructure to Focus On:

- **Digital Systems:** Ensure that your website, e-commerce platform, and digital tools can handle increased traffic and transactions. Invest in scalable hosting, cloud-based systems, and digital security to prevent bottlenecks and downtime as your business grows.
- **Supply Chain and Inventory Management:** If you're selling physical products, scaling your operations means optimizing your supply chain and inventory management. Use inventory management software to track stock levels, automate reordering, and prevent stockouts or overstock.
- **Customer Support:** As you acquire more customers, your customer support systems need to scale with demand. Implement help desk software, live chat, and self-service options to ensure customers can get the help they need quickly and efficiently.
- **Physical Space:** If you operate from a physical location, consider whether your space can accommodate future growth. As you scale, you may need to expand your office, warehouse, or retail space—or move to a new location entirely.

Infrastructure Hustle Tip:

Plan for scalability early. Invest in systems that can grow with your business, so you don't have to constantly overhaul your infrastructure as demand increases.

3. Growing Your Team: Hiring for Scalability

As your business grows, one of the most important areas to focus on is building a strong team that can support and drive your expansion. However, scaling your team isn't just about hiring more people—it's about hiring the right people who align with your company's goals and culture.

Steps to Hire for Scalability:

- **Identify Key Roles:** Start by identifying the roles that will have the greatest impact on your ability to scale. This could be operations, marketing, sales, or customer service. Focus on hiring for these positions first.
- **Hire for Culture Fit:** Skills can be taught, but culture fit is essential to long-term success. Look for candidates who share your company's values and can adapt to a fast-growing, dynamic environment. Employees who are aligned with your mission will be more engaged and invested in your business's success.
- **Onboard and Train Effectively:** A well-structured onboarding and training program is crucial to getting new hires up to speed quickly. Document your processes and provide ongoing training to ensure that your team is fully equipped to handle their responsibilities as you scale.
- **Delegate and Empower:** As you bring on more team members, delegate tasks and responsibilities to them. Trust your team to make decisions and empower them to take ownership of their roles. This frees you up to focus on strategic growth and leadership.

Team Growth Hustle Tip:

Don't rush the hiring process. Take your time to find the right people who are committed to helping you scale and who bring valuable skills to your team.

4. Maintaining Company Culture as You Scale

As your team grows, maintaining a strong company culture becomes more challenging but also more important. A positive, cohesive culture fosters collaboration, innovation, and employee retention—all of which are critical to scaling successfully.

How to Maintain Company Culture:

- **Communicate Your Vision:** Make sure your team is aligned with your company's mission, vision, and values. Regularly communicate these core principles and emphasize how each team member contributes to the bigger picture.
- **Foster Open Communication:** Create an environment where team members feel comfortable sharing ideas, giving feedback, and asking questions. Open communication helps prevent misunderstandings and keeps everyone aligned on company goals.
- **Recognize and Reward Contributions:** As your team grows, it's important to acknowledge individual and collective achievements. Recognize and reward employees who go above and beyond, whether it's through bonuses, promotions, or public recognition.
- **Create Opportunities for Growth:** Offer professional development opportunities, mentorship, and clear paths for advancement within your company. Employees who see opportunities for growth within your organization are more likely to stay committed and motivated.

Culture Hustle Tip:

Lead by example. As the leader of your company, your actions and attitude set the tone for the rest of the team. Demonstrate the values you want to see in your employees, and your company culture will thrive as you scale.

5. Scaling Customer Experience

One of the biggest challenges in scaling operations is maintaining the same level of customer experience that made your business successful in the first place. As you grow, it's crucial to ensure that your customers continue to receive personalized, high-quality service, even as your volume increases.

How to Maintain a Great Customer Experience:

- **Personalize Where Possible:** Even as your customer base grows, look for opportunities to personalize the experience. Use CRM software to track customer preferences, behaviors, and interactions, so you can tailor your communications and offers.
- **Respond Quickly to Feedback:** As your business scales, the volume of customer feedback may increase. Make sure you have systems in place to monitor and respond to customer feedback, whether it's through surveys, reviews, or social media comments.
- **Train Your Team on Customer Service:** Ensure that every member of your team understands the importance of delivering exceptional customer service. Provide ongoing training and create a customer-first mindset throughout the organization.
- **Use Technology to Streamline Support:** Implement technology solutions like live chat, chatbots, and knowledge bases to handle common customer inquiries and support requests. These tools can reduce the burden on your customer support team while ensuring customers get the help they need quickly.

Customer Experience Hustle Tip:

Remember that scaling shouldn't come at the expense of your customer experience. Happy customers are your best source of growth, so make customer satisfaction a top priority as you scale.

6. Managing Finances During Growth

Scaling your operations comes with financial challenges. Growth can be expensive, and managing cash flow is essential to ensuring that your business doesn't overextend itself financially. Proper financial management allows you to scale sustainably while avoiding unnecessary risks.

Financial Strategies for Scaling:

- **Monitor Cash Flow Closely:** As your expenses increase, it's essential to keep a close eye on your cash flow. Make sure you have enough working capital to cover payroll, inventory, marketing, and other operational costs as you scale.

- **Budget for Growth:** Create a detailed budget that outlines your growth plans and the associated costs. This should include hiring, equipment, marketing, and any other expenses related to scaling your business.
- **Explore Funding Options:** If you need additional capital to support your growth, explore funding options like small business loans, angel investors, or venture capital. Be strategic about the type of funding you choose, ensuring it aligns with your long-term goals.
- **Reinvest Profits:** If your business is generating a profit, consider reinvesting those earnings back into the business. Reinvestment allows you to grow without taking on debt or giving up equity.

Finance Hustle Tip:

Stay disciplined with your spending. Just because you have more revenue doesn't mean you should spend it all. Focus on sustainable, strategic investments that will support long-term growth.

7. Monitoring and Measuring Growth

As your business scales, it's important to regularly monitor and measure your progress. Tracking key performance indicators (KPIs) will help you identify areas where you're succeeding and areas where improvements are needed. Data-driven decisions are crucial to scaling effectively.

Key Metrics to Track When Scaling:

- **Revenue Growth:** Track your revenue growth month-over-month and year-over-year. This will give you a clear picture of how quickly your business is growing and whether your scaling efforts are paying off.
- **Customer Acquisition Cost (CAC):** Keep an eye on how much it costs to acquire new customers as you scale. If your CAC is increasing significantly, it may indicate inefficiencies in your marketing or sales processes.
- **Employee Productivity:** Measure productivity across your team to ensure that you're scaling efficiently. This could involve tracking output per employee, sales per representative, or customer service response times.
- **Customer Satisfaction:** Regularly monitor customer satisfaction through surveys, reviews, and feedback. High customer satisfaction is an indicator that you're scaling without sacrificing quality.

Monitoring Hustle Tip:

Use analytics tools to track your KPIs in real time. The more data-driven your decisions are, the more effectively you can scale your operations.

Scaling your operations is one of the most challenging and rewarding aspects of growing a business. By streamlining your processes, building a strong team, and focusing on sustainable growth, you can successfully expand your business while maintaining quality, efficiency, and profitability. Remember, the goal isn't just to grow quickly—it's to grow smartly and sustainably.

Next Chapter: Now that you've learned how to scale your operations, it's time to focus on mastering leadership. In the next chapter, we'll explore how to lead with vision, inspire your team, and navigate the challenges of being an entrepreneurial leader.

Chapter 19

Chapter 19: Mastering Leadership as an Entrepreneur

Leading with Vision, Inspiring Your Team, and Navigating Challenges

Leadership is one of the most critical skills for any entrepreneur, especially as your business grows and your team expands. Leading a company requires more than just managing day-to-day tasks—it involves setting a clear vision, inspiring and motivating your team, and navigating the inevitable challenges that come with growth. Great leaders create an environment where innovation, collaboration, and success thrive.

In this chapter, we'll explore what it takes to become a successful entrepreneurial leader. You'll learn how to define your vision, communicate it effectively, build trust with your team, and foster a culture of accountability and innovation. Leadership isn't just about being in charge—it's about empowering others to excel and achieve shared goals.

1. Defining Your Leadership Style

Every entrepreneur has a unique leadership style, shaped by their personality, values, and experiences. Understanding your leadership style is crucial because it influences how you interact with your team, make decisions, and drive your business forward. There's no one-size-fits-all approach to leadership, but successful leaders are adaptable and self-aware.

Common Leadership Styles:

- **Visionary Leadership:** Visionary leaders inspire their team by setting a clear, long-term direction for the company. They focus on the bigger picture and rally their team around a shared mission. Visionary leaders excel at motivating people, especially during periods of growth or transformation.

- **Servant Leadership:** Servant leaders prioritize the needs of their team above their own. They focus on creating a supportive environment where team members feel valued, empowered, and encouraged to grow. Servant leaders are great at fostering collaboration and loyalty.

- **Autocratic Leadership:** Autocratic leaders make decisions unilaterally, with little input from others. This style can be effective in situations where quick decisions are needed, but it can also stifle creativity and team morale if overused.
- **Democratic Leadership:** Democratic leaders involve their team in the decision-making process. They value input from all members and strive to reach consensus. This leadership style can foster innovation and buy-in from the team, but it may slow down decision-making in fast-paced environments.
- **Transformational Leadership:** Transformational leaders focus on inspiring and motivating their team to achieve extraordinary results. They challenge their team to think creatively, push boundaries, and continuously improve. Transformational leaders are often great at leading through change and driving innovation.

Leadership Hustle Tip:

Your leadership style may evolve as your business grows. Be adaptable and open to refining your approach based on your team's needs and the challenges you face.

2. Setting a Clear Vision and Mission

Great leaders don't just manage tasks—they provide a clear vision for where the company is headed. This vision is the North Star that guides decision-making, goal-setting, and day-to-day operations. Your team needs to know what they're working toward, and it's your job to communicate that vision effectively.

How to Set and Communicate a Vision:

- **Define Your Vision:** What is the long-term goal of your business? What impact do you want to have on your industry or the world? Your vision should be bold, inspiring, and future-focused.
- **Create a Mission Statement:** Your mission statement outlines the core purpose of your business. It answers the question, "Why does this company exist?" A clear mission statement provides direction and helps your team stay aligned with your values and goals.
- **Communicate Regularly:** It's not enough to set a vision once and forget it. Regularly communicate your vision to your team, whether through team meetings, company-wide emails, or one-on-one conversations. Make sure everyone understands how their work contributes to the larger mission.
- **Align Goals with Your Vision:** Ensure that every goal, initiative, and project within your company aligns with your overall vision. This keeps your team focused on what matters and prevents distractions from derailing your progress.

Vision Hustle Tip:

Your vision should be ambitious but achievable. Break it down into smaller milestones to keep your team motivated and on track.

3. Building Trust and Transparency with Your Team

Trust is the foundation of any successful team. Without trust, it's impossible to build a cohesive, high-performing organization. As a leader, it's your responsibility to create an environment where trust thrives—this means being transparent, consistent, and accountable.

How to Build Trust as a Leader:

- **Lead by Example:** Your team will take cues from your actions. If you expect them to work hard, be accountable, and act with integrity, you need to demonstrate those behaviors yourself.
- **Be Transparent:** Share important information with your team, even when it's difficult. Whether it's financial updates, challenges the company is facing, or changes in strategy, transparency builds trust and prevents rumors or misunderstandings from taking hold.
- **Follow Through on Promises:** If you make a commitment to your team, follow through on it. Consistency is key to building trust. If circumstances change and you can't keep a promise, communicate openly and explain why.
- **Encourage Open Communication:** Create a culture where team members feel comfortable sharing their thoughts, ideas, and concerns. Listen actively and take their feedback seriously. When people feel heard, they're more likely to trust their leaders.

Trust Hustle Tip:

Trust is earned over time. Focus on building trust through small, consistent actions, and it will pay off in the long run with a more engaged, loyal team.

4. Empowering Your Team to Take Ownership

Great leaders don't micromanage—they empower their team to take ownership of their roles and responsibilities. Empowered employees are more engaged, motivated, and innovative because they feel trusted to make decisions and contribute meaningfully to the company's success.

How to Empower Your Team:

- **Delegate Responsibility:** Delegation isn't just about offloading tasks—it's about giving your team the authority to make decisions and take ownership of their work. Trust your team to handle important projects, and give them the freedom to experiment and find solutions.
- **Provide the Right Tools and Resources:** Empowerment requires equipping your team with the tools, resources, and training they need to succeed. Make sure they have access to the information and support they need to excel in their roles.

- **Encourage Innovation:** Create an environment where team members feel safe to take risks, share new ideas, and experiment with different approaches. When people feel empowered to innovate, they're more likely to come up with creative solutions that drive the business forward.
- **Recognize and Reward Initiative:** When team members take ownership and go above and beyond, recognize their efforts. Publicly acknowledge their contributions and reward initiative, whether it's through bonuses, promotions, or simply a shout-out in a team meeting.

Empowerment Hustle Tip:

Empowered teams are more resilient and adaptable. When your team feels trusted to make decisions, they'll be more agile and capable of handling challenges without relying on you for every answer.

5. Navigating Challenges and Difficult Decisions

Leadership isn't just about inspiring your team during good times—it's also about navigating challenges and making difficult decisions. Whether it's managing a financial downturn, handling a team conflict, or pivoting your business strategy, effective leaders remain calm, decisive, and focused under pressure.

How to Handle Difficult Decisions:

- **Gather All the Facts:** Before making any major decision, gather as much information as possible. Seek input from your team, advisors, or mentors to get a well-rounded view of the situation.
- **Stay Objective:** It's easy to let emotions cloud your judgment, especially when dealing with high-stakes situations. Stay objective and focus on what's best for the business in the long term, even if it's a tough call in the short term.
- **Communicate Clearly:** Once you've made a decision, communicate it clearly to your team. Explain the reasoning behind your decision, how it aligns with your vision, and what steps will follow. Transparency helps build trust, even when the news is difficult.
- **Stay Resilient:** Leadership requires resilience, especially during tough times. Keep your focus on the bigger picture, and remind your team of the company's vision and long-term goals. Your ability to remain steady under pressure will inspire confidence in your team.

Decision-Making Hustle Tip:

Don't be afraid to make tough decisions. Indecision can be more damaging than making the wrong choice. Once you've made a decision, commit to it and lead with confidence.

6. Fostering a Culture of Accountability

Accountability is essential to creating a high-performing team. When everyone takes ownership of their actions and holds themselves accountable for their work, the entire organization functions more effectively. As a leader, it's your responsibility to set the tone for accountability within your team.

How to Foster Accountability:

- **Set Clear Expectations:** Accountability starts with clear expectations. Make sure every team member knows what's expected of them in terms of performance, behavior, and deliverables.
- **Measure Performance:** Regularly track and measure performance through KPIs, project milestones, and individual goals. Provide feedback on what's going well and where there's room for improvement.
- **Address Issues Directly:** If someone isn't meeting expectations, address the issue directly and promptly. Avoiding difficult conversations only allows problems to fester and negatively impact team morale.
- **Celebrate Accountability:** Recognize and celebrate team members who take ownership and deliver results. When accountability is rewarded, it becomes ingrained in the culture of the organization.

Accountability Hustle Tip:

Lead by example when it comes to accountability. If you make a mistake or fall short of a goal, own it and share what you'll do to improve. This creates a culture where accountability is the norm at every level.

7. Inspiring Innovation and Continuous Improvement

In today's fast-paced business environment, standing still is not an option. Successful leaders inspire their teams to continuously innovate and seek out ways to improve, both personally and professionally. Innovation isn't just about big ideas—it's about fostering a mindset of constant growth and improvement.

How to Inspire Innovation:

- **Encourage Curiosity:** Foster a culture where team members are encouraged to ask questions, challenge assumptions, and explore new ideas. Curiosity leads to innovation, and innovation leads to growth.
- **Create a Safe Space for Failure:** Innovation requires experimentation, and not every experiment will succeed. Create an environment where it's okay to fail, as long as your team learns from the experience and applies those lessons moving forward.
- **Invest in Learning:** Encourage your team to pursue continuous learning and development. Whether it's through workshops, conferences, or online courses, give them the tools and resources to expand their skills and stay ahead of industry trends.
- **Reward Innovation:** Recognize and reward team members who bring innovative ideas to the table. Whether it's a new product idea, a process improvement, or a creative marketing campaign, celebrate the contributions that drive the company forward.

Innovation Hustle Tip:

Make innovation part of your team's regular workflow. Set aside dedicated time for brainstorming sessions, encourage collaboration across departments, and create a process for vetting and implementing new ideas.

Mastering leadership as an entrepreneur is about more than just managing people—it's about inspiring, empowering, and guiding your team to achieve shared goals. By defining a clear vision, building trust, and fostering a culture of accountability and innovation, you'll create a high-performing team that can weather challenges, seize opportunities, and drive your business to new heights.

Next Chapter: Now that you've mastered leadership, it's time to focus on optimizing your company's financials. In the next chapter, we'll dive into managing cash flow, securing funding, and setting your business up for long-term financial success.

20

Chapter 20

Chapter 20: Legacy Building

Creating a Lasting Impact and Planning for the Future

Success in entrepreneurship isn't just about profits or accolades—true success lies in leaving a legacy that endures. Legacy building is about creating lasting impact, influencing others, and ensuring your life's work continues to thrive for future generations. Whether you want to inspire change in your community, lead your industry, or leave behind a meaningful personal brand, legacy building is the ultimate culmination of your hustle.

In this final chapter, we'll delve into how to create a lasting legacy through your business and personal efforts. From empowering others to planning for sustainability, you'll learn how to craft a legacy that reflects your values, your vision, and the long-term goals you want to achieve.

1. Defining Your Legacy

Legacy starts with clarity. Before you can build something that lasts, you need to understand the kind of impact you want to leave behind. Defining your legacy involves reflecting on what's most important to you and your contributions to the world.

How to Define Your Legacy:

- **Identify Your Core Values:** Think about the principles that guide your decisions. What do you want your business to represent? Your legacy should reflect the values you prioritize, whether it's integrity, innovation, social responsibility, or empowerment.
- **Consider Your Community and Industry:** How do you want to be remembered by those in your industry or the communities you've served? Whether you're a pioneer in your field or a champion of underserved communities, the mark you leave behind will shape how people view your contributions.
- **Visualize the Long-Term Impact:** Picture the future of your business and your personal influence. How do you want your work to continue after you're gone? Visualizing your long-term impact helps guide the steps you take today to build that future.

Legacy Hustle Tip:

Your legacy is more than your achievements—it's the lasting influence you have on the people, causes, and communities that matter most to you.

2. Shifting from Success to Significance

While financial success is important, a true legacy is measured by significance—how your work affects others. Building significance means focusing on the long-term value you provide, beyond short-term profits.

How to Build Significance:

- **Incorporate Purpose into Your Business:** Align your business goals with a greater mission. This could mean focusing on social entrepreneurship, addressing pressing issues in your industry, or using your resources to give back to the community.
- **Mentor and Empower Others:** One of the most powerful ways to build a legacy is by passing on your knowledge and experience to others. Mentoring young entrepreneurs, empowering your team, or giving back to future generations ensures your influence continues long after you.
- **Create Sustainable Solutions:** Focus on creating products, services, or systems that offer long-term value. A lasting legacy is built by solutions that stand the test of time, whether through innovation, sustainability, or enduring social impact.

Significance Hustle Tip:

Ask yourself how your business or personal brand can benefit others in the long run. Building significance is about creating value that impacts future generations.

3. Building a Business That Outlives You

A key part of legacy building is ensuring your business can thrive without you at the helm. This involves creating systems, empowering leadership, and structuring your business for long-term success.

Steps to Build a Sustainable Business:

- **Develop Leadership Within Your Organization:** Cultivate a leadership team that shares your vision and values. By empowering others to take the reins, you can ensure that your business continues to grow even after you step away.
- **Establish Clear Systems and Processes:** Build systems that can be followed regardless of who is in charge. Standardizing processes ensures that your business can operate smoothly and efficiently, even as leadership changes.
- **Plan for Succession:** Have a clear succession plan in place. Whether it's passing the business to family members, selling to trusted partners, or transitioning to a nonprofit model, planning for the future ensures that your business's mission and impact remain intact.

Sustainability Hustle Tip:

Your business should be able to function and grow without your day-to-day involvement. Build a structure that can carry your mission forward, even when you're no longer running it.

4. Giving Back to the Community

A strong legacy is often tied to the positive impact you have on the communities around you. Giving back, whether through philanthropy, mentorship, or community involvement, is a meaningful way to ensure your legacy endures.

Ways to Give Back:

- **Invest in Local Initiatives:** Support local causes that align with your values, whether it's education, entrepreneurship, or environmental efforts. By investing in your community, you ensure that your success benefits those around you.
- **Create Social Impact Programs:** Use your business as a vehicle for positive change by implementing social impact initiatives. This could involve launching a scholarship fund, starting a nonprofit, or creating job opportunities in underserved areas.
- **Champion Causes You Care About:** Advocacy and activism can be powerful tools for building your legacy. By championing causes you're passionate about, you can leave a lasting imprint on the social and political issues that matter most to you.

Community Hustle Tip:

Think of giving back as an investment in the future. By supporting your community today, you're helping to shape a better world for tomorrow.

5. Leaving a Legacy of Knowledge

Sharing your knowledge and experiences is one of the most enduring ways to build a legacy. By passing down what you've learned, you empower others to succeed and create a ripple effect that extends far beyond your immediate influence.

How to Share Your Knowledge:

- **Write a Book or Blog:** Document your journey, your lessons, and your insights for others to learn from. Whether it's a business book, a memoir, or a blog, sharing your experiences helps future entrepreneurs avoid the same mistakes and replicate your successes.
- **Speak and Teach:** Consider giving talks, leading workshops, or teaching courses in your area of expertise. By sharing your knowledge with others, you inspire the next generation of leaders and entrepreneurs.
- **Create Educational Resources:** Develop online courses, webinars, or podcasts to share your expertise on a larger scale. These resources can reach people around the world and provide lasting value long after they're created.

Knowledge Legacy Tip:

Your knowledge is one of your greatest assets. Share it freely to ensure that your ideas, insights, and values continue to influence others long after you're gone.

6. Planning for the Future

A true legacy requires planning. This means thinking beyond the day-to-day operations of your business and setting long-term goals for how your work and impact will continue after you're no longer involved.

Steps to Plan for the Future:

- **Create a Long-Term Vision:** What do you want your business and personal impact to look like in 10, 20, or 50 years? A long-term vision will guide your decisions and ensure that you're always building toward a lasting legacy.
- **Establish a Trust or Foundation:** Many entrepreneurs set up trusts or foundations to manage their wealth and ensure it is used to support causes they care about after they're gone. This can be a powerful way to ensure your resources continue to make a difference.
- **Set Up a Charitable Giving Plan:** Whether through your business or personal finances, create a charitable giving plan that supports the causes and communities you care about. This ensures that your success continues to benefit others even after you've passed the torch.

Future Hustle Tip:

Legacy building is about the long game. Plan strategically for the future to ensure that your work, values, and impact continue to grow and inspire others.

Building a legacy is about more than just your business—it's about creating lasting value, empowering others, and making a meaningful impact on the world. By focusing on significance, sustainability, and giving back, you can ensure that your hustle leaves a mark that endures for generations.

Conclusion:

The journey from hustler to legacy builder is a long and rewarding one. Every step you've taken, from building your brand to overcoming setbacks, has prepared you to leave a lasting impact. Now, it's time to focus on the future—creating a legacy that will inspire others and stand the test of time.

II
Part Two

Conclusion

Conclusion: The Hustler's Journey

Embracing the Path to Lasting Success

Entrepreneurship is a journey, and as a hustler, you know that the path to success isn't always smooth. It's filled with challenges, setbacks, and moments of doubt. But it's also a journey of growth, opportunity, and achievement. This book has laid out the essential plays for building a thriving business, developing your personal brand, navigating the financial jungle, and scaling your hustle into something greater than you ever imagined. Now, it's up to you to put those plays into action.

Throughout this journey, you've learned the importance of resilience, creativity, and adaptability. You've discovered that every setback is an opportunity to learn, and that success is not just about working hard—it's about working smart, building connections, and staying true to your vision. The hustle is more than just a grind; it's a mindset and a way of life that empowers you to take control of your destiny.

The Power of Perseverance

One of the most valuable lessons in this book is that perseverance is the key to overcoming obstacles. The most successful hustlers are the ones who refuse to give up, even when the odds are stacked against them. Whether you're bootstrapping your business, dealing with financial setbacks, or navigating uncharted industries, remember that your persistence is what will set you apart.

Success doesn't happen overnight. It's the result of consistent effort, a willingness to pivot, and the determination to keep moving forward, no matter the challenges you face. Keep pushing, keep adapting, and never lose sight of your long-term goals.

Innovation and Adaptability: The Keys to Staying Ahead

In a rapidly changing world, the ability to innovate and adapt is crucial. As you continue to grow your business, remember that the most successful entrepreneurs are those who can anticipate change and respond to it proactively. This means staying ahead of trends, embracing new technologies, and continuously refining your strategies.

Innovation isn't just about coming up with new ideas—it's about being willing to take risks and try new things, even when the path forward isn't clear. Be fearless in your pursuit of growth, and don't be afraid to reinvent yourself or your business when necessary. The most successful entrepreneurs are those who evolve with the times while staying true to their core values.

The Importance of Giving Back

As your business grows and you achieve success, remember the importance of giving back to your community. Whether through mentorship, supporting other entrepreneurs, or reinvesting in underserved communities, your impact can extend far beyond your business. Building a legacy means not only achieving personal success but also contributing to the success of others.

When you give back, you strengthen the ecosystem that supports your business and create a positive ripple effect. By empowering others, you're building a foundation for long-term, sustainable success, not just for yourself but for the next generation of entrepreneurs.

Your Legacy: Building Something That Lasts

The ultimate goal of any hustler is to create something lasting—something that outlives the day-to-day grind and continues to have an impact long after you're gone. Whether it's a thriving business, a personal brand, or a community initiative, your legacy is the mark you leave on the world.

Think about the legacy you want to build. What values do you want to pass on? How do you want to be remembered? As you continue on your entrepreneurial journey, keep your legacy in mind and make decisions that align with your long-term vision. Every choice you make, every risk you take, and every challenge you overcome is part of building that lasting impact.

The Journey Continues

While this book has provided you with the tools and strategies to succeed, your journey as a hustler is far from over. The world of entrepreneurship is constantly evolving, and there will always be new opportunities and challenges to face. Stay curious, stay hungry, and continue learning as you grow your business and brand.

Above all, remember that success is not just about reaching a destination—it's about the journey itself. Embrace the hustle, trust in your abilities, and keep moving forward with confidence and purpose. The future is yours to shape.

Thank You for Hustling

Thank you for taking the time to invest in yourself and your business by reading this book. The hustle is not easy, but with the right mindset, tools, and strategies, it's possible to achieve your goals and create a lasting impact. Now it's time to get out there, execute the plays, and build the future you've envisioned.

Glossary for I Got a Play for You: A Hustler's Handbook for Serial Entrepreneurs

Glossary for *I Got a Play for You: A Hustler's Handbook for Serial Entrepreneurs*

Accelerator:

A program designed to fast-track the growth of startups through mentorship, resources, and sometimes funding, often culminating in a demo day where entrepreneurs pitch to investors.

Advisory Board:

A group of experienced individuals who provide strategic advice and guidance to a business without formal governance responsibilities. Advisory boards often help entrepreneurs navigate growth, challenges, and key decisions.

Angel Investor:

An individual who provides financial backing to startups in exchange for equity ownership. Angel investors typically invest in early-stage companies and often offer mentorship along with funding.

B2B (Business-to-Business):

A business model where a company sells its products or services to other businesses, rather than to individual consumers (B2C).

B2C (Business-to-Consumer):

A business model in which a company sells its products or services directly to consumers, rather than to other businesses.

Bootstrapping:

Building a business from the ground up with little to no external funding, often relying on personal savings, reinvesting profits, and maximizing cost-effective strategies.

Burn Rate:

The rate at which a startup spends its cash before generating positive cash flow. This metric is particularly important for businesses that rely on external funding and need to manage their resources carefully.

Business Plan:

A comprehensive document that outlines the goals, strategies, target market, financial projections, and operational plan for a business. It is often used to attract investors and guide growth.

Capital Expenditure (CapEx):

Money spent by a business to acquire or maintain fixed assets such as buildings, machinery, or technology. CapEx investments typically have a long-term impact on the business.

Churn Rate:

The percentage of customers who stop using a company's product or service during a given period, often used to measure customer retention in subscription-based businesses.

Competitive Advantage:

The unique strengths or benefits that give a company an edge over its competitors, often related to product quality, cost structure, branding, or customer service.

Conversion Rate:

The percentage of website visitors or leads who take a specific action, such as making a purchase or signing up for a newsletter. This is a key metric in digital marketing.

Crowdfunding:

A method of raising small amounts of money from a large number of people, typically through online platforms. Crowdfunding is often used by startups to fund projects, products, or services without relying on traditional investors.

Customer Acquisition Cost (CAC):

The total cost of acquiring a new customer, including marketing, sales, and other expenses, divided by the number of customers gained. It helps businesses assess the efficiency of their growth strategies.

Customer Lifetime Value (CLTV):

The total revenue a business expects to generate from a single customer over the duration of their relationship, used to assess the long-term profitability of acquiring and retaining customers.

Disruptive Innovation:

An innovation that creates a new market or significantly alters an existing one, displacing established companies and products. Disruptive innovations are often initially overlooked but eventually reshape industries.

Due Diligence:

The process of thoroughly investigating a business before entering into a deal, merger, acquisition, or investment. It includes assessing financial records, legal matters, market conditions, and operational performance.

Elevator Pitch:

A concise, compelling description of a business or idea that can be delivered in the time it takes to ride an elevator, usually 30 seconds to two minutes. It's used to quickly capture interest from investors, partners, or clients.

Equity:

Ownership in a company, typically represented by shares. Investors, founders, and employees can hold equity in exchange for their contributions or investments.

Exit Strategy:

A plan for how an entrepreneur or investor will realize a return on investment, typically by selling the company, merging with another company, or going public through an initial public offering (IPO).

Franchise:

A business model where a company (franchisor) grants an individual or company (franchisee) the rights to operate a business using its brand, systems, and support in exchange for fees or royalties.

Guerrilla Marketing:

An unconventional and low-cost marketing strategy designed to achieve maximum exposure using creative, attention-grabbing tactics, often relying on viral or word-of-mouth spread.

Intellectual Property (IP):

Legal rights protecting creations of the mind, such as inventions (patents), literary and artistic works (copyrights), designs (design patents), and symbols or names (trademarks) used in commerce.

Lean Startup:

A business methodology that emphasizes creating a minimum viable product (MVP), testing it with real customers, and rapidly iterating based on feedback to reduce waste and increase the likelihood of success.

Liquidity:

The ability of a business to quickly convert assets into cash without affecting the asset's price. Liquidity is crucial for managing short-term financial obligations and operational flexibility.

Market Penetration:

A measure of how much a product or service has been adopted by customers in its target market, expressed as a percentage. It's often used to assess the success of marketing efforts and product acceptance.

Minimum Viable Product (MVP):

A version of a product with just enough features to be usable by early customers, allowing businesses to gather feedback and validate assumptions before investing in full-scale development.

Networking:

The process of building and maintaining professional relationships to create business opportunities, share knowledge, and gain access to new markets or resources.

Pivot:

A significant change in a company's business model, strategy, or product offering in response to market feedback or challenges, often aimed at improving chances of success.

Revenue Model:

A business's plan for generating income. Common revenue models include product sales, subscriptions, licensing, advertising, and transaction fees.

Scalability:

The capacity of a business to grow and increase its output or customer base without being constrained by its current structure, resources, or operational processes.

Seed Funding:

The initial capital raised by a startup to develop its product, test the market, and build the business before seeking larger investments. Seed funding typically comes from angel investors, friends, family, or crowdfunding.

Sweat Equity:

The non-monetary investment made by founders or team members, such as time, effort, and expertise, in exchange for ownership or shares in a company.

Target Market:

A specific group of consumers that a business aims to serve with its products or services, identified by demographic, geographic, or behavioral characteristics.

Venture Capital:

Investment funds provided by venture capital firms to startups and early-stage companies with high growth potential, typically in exchange for equity and a role in guiding the company's development.

Resource Apps and Platforms for I Got a Play for You: A Hustler's Handbook for Serial Entrepreneurs

Resource Apps and Platforms for I Got a Play for You: A Hustler's Handbook for Serial Entrepreneurs

Project Management:

1. **Trello:**
2. A visual project management tool that uses boards, lists, and cards to help organize tasks and track progress. Ideal for entrepreneurs managing multiple projects or teams.
3. *Website:* https://trello.com
4. **Asana:**
5. A project management platform that allows you to assign tasks, set deadlines, and collaborate with team members. Great for tracking the progress of larger projects.
6. *Website:* https://asana.com
7. **Monday.com:**
8. A highly customizable project management tool that helps teams collaborate, plan projects, and automate workflows.
9. *Website:* https://monday.com

Team Communication:

1. **Slack:**
2. A messaging app for teams that allows for real-time communication, file sharing, and integrations with other tools. Ideal for remote teams and efficient communication.
3. *Website:* https://slack.com
4. **Microsoft Teams:**
5. A collaboration platform that includes chat, video meetings, file sharing, and integration with Microsoft Office tools, ideal for businesses that already use Office 365.
6. *Website:* https://www.microsoft.com/en-us/microsoft-teams
7. **Zoom:**
8. A video conferencing tool that enables virtual meetings, webinars, and screen sharing, making it ideal for team collaboration and client communication.
9. *Website:* https://zoom.us

Accounting and Finance:

1. **QuickBooks:**
2. An accounting software for small businesses that helps manage income, expenses, and payroll, with options for invoicing, tracking cash flow, and generating reports.
3. *Website:* https://quickbooks.intuit.com
4. **Wave:**
5. A free accounting platform designed for entrepreneurs and small businesses. It offers tools for invoicing, bookkeeping, and receipt scanning.
6. *Website:* https://www.waveapps.com
7. **FreshBooks:**
8. A cloud accounting solution tailored for freelancers and small businesses, offering invoicing, expense tracking, and time tracking.
9. *Website:* https://www.freshbooks.com

Marketing Tools:

1. **Canva:**
2. A graphic design platform that allows users to create social media graphics, presentations, posters, and more with a simple drag-and-drop interface.
3. *Website:* https://www.canva.com
4. **Hootsuite:**
5. A social media management platform that allows you to schedule posts, manage multiple accounts, and track engagement metrics across social platforms.
6. *Website:* https://hootsuite.com
7. **Mailchimp:**
8. An all-in-one email marketing tool that allows you to design email campaigns, automate messaging, and track performance. Perfect for small businesses starting out in email marketing.
9. *Website:* https://mailchimp.com

E-Commerce Platforms:

1. **Shopify:**
2. An all-in-one e-commerce platform that enables entrepreneurs to build and customize their online store, manage inventory, and sell products globally.
3. *Website:* https://www.shopify.com
4. **Etsy:**
5. A marketplace tailored for handmade, vintage, and unique products. Perfect for creative entrepreneurs looking to reach a broad audience without setting up a dedicated e-commerce site.

6. *Website:* https://www.etsy.com
7. **BigCommerce:**
8. An e-commerce solution designed for growing brands that need scalability, offering robust features, customizable themes, and integrations with major payment providers.
9. *Website:* https://www.bigcommerce.com

Crowdfunding Platforms:

1. **Kickstarter:**
2. A crowdfunding platform for creative projects, helping entrepreneurs raise money by offering backers rewards for their support.
3. *Website:* https://www.kickstarter.com
4. **Indiegogo:**
5. A crowdfunding platform that supports entrepreneurs, nonprofits, and individuals with both fixed and flexible funding options for campaigns.
6. *Website:* https://www.indiegogo.com
7. **GoFundMe:**
8. A donation-based crowdfunding platform ideal for community-focused projects, nonprofit ventures, or personal fundraising efforts.
9. *Website:* https://www.gofundme.com

Customer Relationship Management (CRM):

1. **HubSpot CRM:**
2. A free CRM platform that helps businesses organize customer interactions, track sales leads, and automate follow-ups. HubSpot also offers advanced marketing tools.
3. *Website:* https://www.hubspot.com
4. **Zoho CRM:**
5. An affordable CRM tool designed for small businesses, offering lead management, sales automation, and real-time analytics.
6. *Website:* https://www.zoho.com/crm

Legal & Compliance Tools:

1. **LegalZoom:**
2. An online platform that provides legal services for businesses, including forming LLCs, drafting contracts, and trademark registration.
3. *Website:* https://www.legalzoom.com
4. **Rocket Lawyer:**

5. A service that offers legal document creation, attorney consultations, and business formation assistance for entrepreneurs and small businesses.
6. *Website:* https://www.rocketlawyer.com
7. **DocuSign:**
8. An e-signature solution that allows you to sign, send, and manage contracts and agreements securely online.
9. *Website:* https://www.docusign.com

Freelancer and Gig Platforms:

1. **Upwork:**
2. A global freelancing platform where businesses can hire freelancers for various tasks, from design and marketing to development and customer service.
3. *Website:* https://www.upwork.com
4. **Fiverr:**
5. An online marketplace where freelancers offer services across different categories, from graphic design and writing to digital marketing and programming, typically starting at $5.
6. *Website:* https://www.fiverr.com

Payment Processing:

1. **Stripe:**
2. A payment processing platform for online businesses, allowing them to accept credit cards, debit cards, and other forms of payment.
3. *Website:* https://stripe.com
4. **PayPal:**
5. A trusted payment processing platform for small businesses, offering tools for invoicing, payment processing, and online transactions.
6. *Website:* https://www.paypal.com

Networking and Event Platforms:

1. **Eventbrite:**
2. An event management and ticketing platform that allows entrepreneurs to organize, promote, and sell tickets for events, workshops, and seminars.
3. *Website:* https://www.eventbrite.com
4. **Meetup:**
5. A platform for organizing in-person and virtual events centered around shared interests, industries, and networking opportunities. Great for building connections and growing a business community.

6. *Website:* https://www.meetup.com

About the Author

Also by Conceptualize Writer